I0105715

Broken Promises

The Freedom Charter's Dream Gone South

From Promise to Crisis: How Governance Choices Undermined
South Africa's Democratic Transition

Robert Mzimela

Copyright ©2025 Robert Mzimela

All rights reserved.

No part of this book may be reproduced or transmitted in any form or by any electronic means, including photocopying and recording, without written permission from the publisher.

Paperback ISBN: 978-1-971854-03-8

Book Cover Design: Creative SA

Edited by Creative Books SA

Layout & Typesetting by Creative Books SA

Ghost Writer: Nomaphelo Precious Madiba

This book is dedicated to the people who shaped and supported me throughout my life. First and foremost, I thank my wife and children, whose constant encouragement inspired me to write this book — especially my daughter, Dr. Ntokozo Mzimela.

I am deeply grateful to my late aunt, Mehlathathane Shembe, who raised me and taught me the value of hard work. I also acknowledge Prince Mangosuthu Buthelezi, who served as my minister during my time as Secretary of the former KwaZulu Legislative Assembly; his guidance had a profound influence on my career.

My gratitude extends to Mr. T.C. Memela, Mrs. Zodwa Buthelezi and her late husband, the father of Thulasizwe Buthelezi. I would also like to thank Mr. Themba Zuma of Maphumulo, who freely offered his help in building my home.

To my late brother, Mdedeleni Nicholas Mzimela — thank you for encouraging me to pursue my university studies. I also remember Reverend Z.A. Khanyile & Pat Nyandu, my close friends through many years.

Lastly, I thank all the former staff of the KwaZulu Legislative Assembly for their support during my tenure as Secretary and I owe special thanks to Nomaphelo P. Madiba, who worked closely with me in conceiving and shaping this book. Without her dedication, this work would not have been possible.

Prologue

The rebirth of South Africa in 1994 came with innumerable challenges. It has been exactly 31 years since we had a democratic president in our country, and we will highlight the transition and the baby steps we took that landed us where we are now.

The transition came with a lot of responsibilities for every South African to take care of the country, and the government's responsibility to work together with the people in solidarity.

According to the Freedom Charter, our country belongs to all of us, and everyone who lives here. It is unfortunate that we have transferred our birthrights to everyone else, and we live like visitors or tenants in our own country.

As we delve into the present state, it is important for us to understand history, so that we understand why things are done the way they are, and what we can do to make it a better place for you, for me and the new generation that is still growing up and those that are yet to be born, and who do not have the slightest idea of what is happening.

Let us sit together to analyse the causes of the downfall of our country, and we must not pretend that we do not care. It is essential for us to proceed with care as we conduct the analysis and identify areas for improvement.

They say a journey of a thousand miles begins with just one step. We don't have solutions for the breakdown, but the little knowledge that we will share will have an influence on one or two people, and they might influence their one or two people. Before we know it, we have influenced a hundred people, then a million.

I hope as you read, your mind will be opened, and you will have your own life's blueprint. Martin Luther King Jr. asked a very pivotal question: "What is your life's blueprint?".

I hope this book will also become part of your reference as you decide how to live your life moving forward.

A Note to the Reader

This book is dedicated to the young, the old, and to every South African. It is written from the experiences of a patriot, someone who has the best interests of the country at heart. It is dedicated to every South African who continues to strive for the ideals enshrined in the Freedom Charter, and to those who fought and sacrificed for the promise of a better future.

One person said, if you were sitting in a ship that was at risk of sinking because you had noticed a small hole on your way in, would you sit and hope someone else would notice and mend it? Or would you scream at the top of your voice and say, there is a hole in this ship, help! Just like you would shout and scream at the top of your voice on that ship, it is everyone's responsibility to scream and do something as we see our dear country sinking.

We are nowhere near where we need to be, but together we can put South Africa first by fighting for what is left of it.

To the religious groups, let us pray for the country, for the children, for the future, and for our leaders. We may not all believe this, but prayer changes things. This is the time to come together and sing together in one accord, just like we did in the time of Covid, when we were losing family members, friends and colleagues, we sang, "*If you believe and I believe, and we pray together, the holy spirit shall come down and Africa will be saved!*".

I remember how we sat in our homes in despair as we woke up to the new number of people that died, may all their souls find eternal peace.

Patriots let us fight, and never lose hope, no matter what.

Please read this book with an open mind, and it is in no way condemning any group of people or parties, but it focuses on how we can make South Africa great again.

To assist the reader, we will provide explanations for all abbreviations.

May you enjoy reading this book, but for the most part, may you learn a thing or two and may you see how you can add value to this country as you navigate through the collapse of our economy, remember that if you remove one rand from a million rand, it becomes 999 999, you may think your voice is insignificant, but remember this, your voice counts, your vote counts, your contribution counts.

Foreword

About Mrs Zodwa Buthelezi

My name is Mrs Zodwa Buthelezi. I was married to the late Reverend Buthelezi, a man of God who served our community with great love and dedication. We were blessed with children, including our son, Reverend Thulasizwe Buthelezi, who now serves as the MEC of Cooperative Governance and Traditional Affairs (COGTA) in KwaZulu-Natal. As a pastor's wife, I had the privilege of meeting many people in our community and witnessing the changes that shaped our province over the years.

Remembering "The Government" – Mr Mzimela

I want to tell you about Mr. Mzimela, a man who was very powerful in the KwaZulu Government. This was when KwaZulu was its own territory inside South Africa, from 1975 to 1994. Mr. Mzimela worked closely with Chief Minister Mangosuthu Buthelezi. But when democracy came in 1994, everything changed.

I first met Mr Mzimela in 1984. I knew him both at home and through government work. At home, I became close friends with his wife, MaZulu uMntwana, who is a princess. She was and still is a beautiful lady with a daunting figure and the most beautiful heart.

In 1985, I went to the opening of the KwaZulu Government meeting in Ulundi. I knew very little about politics or who held which jobs. I did not know then that Mr. Mzimela was the secretary of the KwaZulu Government. After 1994, he became the secretary of the KwaZulu-Natal Legislature.

During these government meetings, Mr Mzimela sat in a big chair at the front where everyone could see him. He was a leader with great authority. He was tall, big, and strong. Because of how he looked and his important job, people called him "Uhulumeni" – which means "The Government."

In the 1970s and 1980s, many black people did not understand politics. We always heard about "Uhulumeni" – The Government. This was the person who made all the rules we had to follow. We wanted to see what this person looked like. We imagined he must be a big, tall, strong man.

When we saw Mr Mzimela, he looked exactly like what we thought "The Government" should look like. We were happy to have "Uhulumeni" living among us.

At home, Mr. Mzimela was a good family man with a wife and children. He was kind, generous, and welcoming to his neighbours. He worked hard on his farm. His vegetable garden fed many families. As a pastor's wife, I received plenty of food from him for free.

When Everything Changed

Every year, I went to the opening of the government meetings in Ulundi. Mr Mzimela was always there, doing his job with pride. In 1994, we voted for the first time. Democracy began – a new time for our country. We were excited and hoped for good things. Changes did happen, but not the ones we expected. Ulundi changed completely.

All the government offices moved to Pietermaritzburg. The legislature also moved to Pietermaritzburg. Families were separated as husbands, wives, and children were sent to different locations. Old friends lost touch with each other – this is how I lost contact with the Mzimela family.

Old ways of doing things disappeared. I stopped attending government meetings in Pietermaritzburg. The workers stopped wearing nice clothes like suits and ties for men and smart dresses with high heels for women. People came to work wearing t-shirts and jeans. You could not distinguish between workers and visitors.

The offices in Ulundi became empty. The big family houses and government houses were left vacant. Many houses were broken into and damaged. The places looked bad. The gardens were not looked after like before, when Mr Leech took care of them. Cows and goats wandered into the office buildings. Ulundi looked like a ghost town.

Airplanes stopped flying between Ulundi, Pietermaritzburg, and Durban. When you drove off the highway to Ulundi, you hardly saw any cars. It was scary to drive alone on those empty roads. Local factories closed down. All the beautiful places, people, and life we knew disappeared.

For people who moved from Ulundi to Pietermaritzburg, life was hard. Many left their jobs early because they were unable to cope.

What happened to our beloved "Uhulumeni," Mr Mzimela, the secretary of the KwaZulu-Natal Legislature? His story shows us how big promises were broken, and how dreams of freedom took a different path than we expected.

This is why this book is called "Broken Promises: The Freedom Charter's Dream Gone South." It tells the truth about what really happened to ordinary people when everything changed.

Mrs. Zodwa Buthelezi *Foreword to "Broken Promises: The Freedom Charter's Dream Gone South"*

Table of Contents

Introduction

The book shall focus on the Freedom Charter, and it is only fair to quote it as it is, rather than to paraphrase it.

Overview of the Freedom Charter: Its Vision and Significance

The Charter is organized around ten key principles:

Adopted at the Congress of the People, Kliptown, on 26 June 1955

We, the People of South Africa, declare for all our country and the world to know:

that South Africa belongs to all who live in it, black and white, and that no government can justly claim authority unless it is based on the will of all the people.

that our people have been robbed of their birthright to land, liberty and peace by a form of government founded on injustice and inequality.

that our country will never be prosperous or free until all our people live in brotherhood, enjoying equal rights and opportunities; that only a democratic state, based on the will of all the people, can secure to all their birthright without distinction of colour, race, sex or belief; And therefore, we, the people of South Africa, black and white together equals,

1

countrymen and brothers adopt this Freedom Charter; And we pledge ourselves to strive together, sparing neither strength nor courage, until the democratic changes here set out have been won.

✓ *The People Shall Govern!*

Every man and woman shall have the right to vote for and to stand as a candidate for all bodies which make laws; All people shall be entitled to take part in the administration of the country; The rights of the people shall be the same, regardless of race, colour or sex; All bodies of minority rule, advisory boards, councils and authorities shall be replaced by democratic organs of self-government.

✓ *All National Groups shall have Equal Rights!*

There shall be equal status in the bodies of state, in the courts and in the schools for all national groups and races; All people shall have equal right to use their own languages, and to develop their own folk culture and customs; All national groups shall be protected by law against insults to their race and national pride; The preaching and practice of national, race or colour discrimination and contempt shall be a punishable crime; All apartheid laws and practices shall be set aside.

✓ *The People Shall Share in the Country's Wealth!*

The national wealth of our country, the heritage of South Africans, shall be restored to the people; The mineral wealth beneath the soil, the Banks and monopoly industry shall be transferred to the ownership of the people as a whole; All other industry and trade shall be controlled to assist the wellbeing of the people; All people shall have equal rights to trade where they choose, to manufacture and to enter all trades, crafts and professions.

✓ *The Land Shall be Shared Among Those Who Work It!*

Restrictions of land ownership on a racial basis shall be ended, and all the land re-divided amongst those who work it to banish famine and land hunger; The state shall help the peasants with implements, seed, tractors and dams to save the soil and assist the tillers; Freedom of movement shall be guaranteed to all who work on the land; All shall have the right to occupy land wherever they choose; People shall not be robbed of their cattle, and forced labour and farm prisons shall be abolished.

✓ *All Shall be Equal Before the Law!*

No one shall be imprisoned, deported or restricted without a fair trial; no one shall be condemned by the order of any Government official; The courts shall be representative of all the people; Imprisonment shall be only for serious crimes against the people, and shall aim at re-education, not vengeance.

The police force and army shall be open to all on an equal basis and shall be the helpers and protectors of the people; All laws which discriminate on grounds of race, colour or belief shall be repealed.

Robert Mzimela

✓ *All Shall Enjoy Equal Human Rights!*

The law shall guarantee to all their right to speak, to organise, to meet together, to publish, to preach, to worship and to educate their children; The privacy of the house from police raids shall be protected by law; All shall be free to travel without restriction from countryside to town, from province to province, and from South Africa abroad; Pass Laws, permits and all other laws restricting these freedoms shall be abolished.

✓ *There Shall be Work and Security!*

All who work shall be free to form trade unions, to elect their officers and to make wage agreements with their employers; The state shall recognise the right and duty of all to work, and to draw full unemployment benefits; Men and women of all races shall receive equal pay for equal work; There shall be a forty-hour working week, a national minimum wage, paid annual leave, and sick leave for all workers, and maternity leave on full pay for all working mothers;

Miners, domestic workers, farm workers and civil servants shall have the same rights as all others who work; Child labour, compound labour, the tot system and contract labour shall be abolished.

✓ *The Doors of Learning and Culture Shall be Opened!*

The government shall discover, develop and encourage national talent for the enhancement of our cultural life; All the cultural treasures of mankind shall be open to all, by free exchange of books, ideas and contact with other lands.

The aim of education shall be to teach the youth to love their people and their culture, to honour human brotherhood, liberty and peace; Education shall be free, compulsory, universal and equal for all children.

Higher education and technical training shall be opened to all by means of state allowances and scholarships awarded on the basis of merit; Adult illiteracy shall be ended by a mass state education plan; Teachers shall have all the rights of other citizens; The colour bar in cultural life, in sport and in education shall be abolished.

✓ **There Shall be Houses, Security and Comfort!**

All people shall have the right to live where they choose, be decently housed, and to bring up their families in comfort and security; Unused housing space to be made available to the people; Rent and prices shall be lowered, food plentiful, and no one shall go hungry; A preventive health scheme shall be run by the state.

Free medical care and hospitalisation shall be provided for all, with special care for mothers and young children; slums shall be demolished, and new suburbs built where all have transport, roads, lighting, playing fields, creches and social centres; The aged, the orphans, the disabled and the sick shall be cared for by the state; Rest, leisure and recreation shall be the right of all: Fenced locations and ghettoes shall be abolished, and laws which break up families shall be repealed.

✓ **There Shall be Peace and Friendship!**

South Africa shall be a fully independent state which respects the rights and sovereignty of all nations; South Africa shall strive to maintain world peace and the settlement of all international disputes by negotiation, not war; Peace and friendship amongst all our people shall be secured by upholding the equal rights, opportunities and status of all.

The people of the protectorates Basutoland, Bechuanaland and Swaziland shall be free to decide for themselves their own future; The right of all peoples of Africa to independence and self-government shall be recognised and shall be the basis of close co-operation. Let all people who love their people and their country now say, as we say here: THESE FREEDOMS WE WILL FIGHT FOR, SIDE BY SIDE, THROUGHOUT OUR LIVES, UNTIL WE HAVE WON OUR LIBERTY

The Promise of democracy in South Africa

Introduction

In 1994, South Africa entered a new era with the end of apartheid and the establishment of a democratic system, underpinned by the 1996 Constitution. For the first time, all citizens, regardless of race, could vote and participate equally in the political process. This marked the realization of promises communicated in the *Freedom Charter* of 1955, which declared that *"The People Shall Govern."* Democracy in

South Africa carries the promise of freedom, equality, dignity, and justice for all its people.

1. Political Equality and Representation

Democracy promised that every South African would have an equal voice. Universal right to vote meant that Black South Africans, who were excluded under apartheid, could elect representatives and hold leaders accountable. The proportional representation system was designed to ensure that even smaller parties could secure seats in Parliament, thereby reflecting the diversity of society.

2. Protection of Rights and Freedoms

The Constitution preserves one of the most progressive Bills of Rights in the world. It guarantees rights to freedom of expression, association, religion, movement, and political participation. Importantly, it also secures socio-economic rights such as access to housing, healthcare, and education, linking democracy to social justice.

3. Social and Economic Justice

Democracy was not only going to end political oppression but also to dismantle the deep inequality created by apartheid. Policies such as affirmative action, land reform, and Black Economic Empowerment (BEE) were introduced to broaden access to resources and opportunities. The democratic state carried the promise of reducing poverty, creating jobs, and ensuring a fairer distribution of wealth. The promise of democracy in South Africa is not just about the right to vote but about building a society built on equality, dignity, and justice. Although the journey is incomplete and challenged by structural setbacks, the democratic system remains a beacon of hope. It provides the foundation upon which South Africa can continue striving to realize the vision of the *Freedom Charter*: a country where all people truly govern.

Key Principles and Aspirations of the Charter

The Freedom Charter begins with the declaration that "South Africa belongs to all who live in it, black and white, and that no government can justly claim authority unless it is based on the will of all the people". This radical statement directly challenged the foundations of apartheid and set forth a vision of a non-racial democracy.

The Freedom Charter emerged during one of the darkest periods of South African history. By the mid-1950s, the apartheid system had become firmly established, systematically denying basic rights and dignity to the majority of South Africans. The Population Registration Act (1950), the Group Areas Act (1950), and the Bantu Education Act (1953) formed part of a comprehensive legislative framework designed to enforce racial segregation and white supremacy.

It was against this backdrop that the Congress Alliance, comprising the African National Congress (ANC), the South African Indian Congress, the South African Congress of Democrats, and the Coloured People's Congress, launched the Congress of the People campaign. The campaign called upon South Africans from all walks of life to submit their demands for the kind of South Africa they wanted to live in.

Thousands of volunteers went into towns, villages, and rural areas across the country, collecting the demands and aspirations of ordinary people. These demands, written on scraps of paper, were then gathered and formulated into what would become the Freedom Charter.

On June 26, 1955, more than 3,000 delegates gathered at the Congress of the People in Kliptown, Soweto. Despite police intimidation and surveillance, the delegates adopted the Freedom Charter, clause by clause. The meeting was eventually disrupted by police, who confiscated documents and recorded the names of attendees. However, the Freedom Charter had already been born, and it would go on to inspire generations of freedom fighters.

Chapter 1

The Legacy of the Freedom Charter

Historical Context and the Birth of the Charter

The freedom charter was born out of the collective consultations and vision of a new, united South Africa which aimed to present a nonracial, and non-biased democratic country that enjoyed equal rights and opportunities, it holds a very profound legacy because when South Africa formed the constitution and the bill of rights in 1996, the foundation was the freedom charter, to this day, we still enjoy some of the visions the charter aimed to achieve.

As many of us know, black people were denied many opportunities and basic human rights; the charter turned a lot of those things around, because black people were then allowed to vote and enjoy some of the benefits that their white counterparts enjoyed. Please do note that the term "black" in the South African context refers to every racial group that is non-white. This refers to a group of people who were previously disadvantaged.

The Freedom Charter was born at the Congress of the People, where over 3,000 delegates from diverse backgrounds, including workers, servants, students, and intellectuals from all racial groups, were brought together.

One of the most misused lines from the charter is, "South Africa belongs to those who live in it". I am certain that when it was quoted, it had a different connotation than it does today. As we will expand on this further in the book, we will explain why that line is concerning.

We must acknowledge the formation of the Freedom Charter because it was a powerful force that served as a tool to liberate the marginalized group, and it served as a reference and a guiding document for many political parties. To this day, we cannot speak of the liberation without quoting the Freedom Charter.

Aspirations of the Charter

The main role of the charter is to readdress the past and to rewrite history by correcting the unfairness that was caused by apartheid.

These principles represented not only a rejection of apartheid but also a complete vision for a democratic, equal, and just society. The Charter's influence extended far beyond

South Africa, inspiring liberation movements across the continent and around the world.

The Freedom Charter's legacy lies not only in its role in the struggle against apartheid but

also, in its continuing relevance to modern-day South Africa. It remains a measure for

inspecting the country's progress and social justice, and it remains as a memento of the promises that have yet to be fulfilled.

In the chapters that follow, we will examine how South Africa has experienced setbacks in realizing these

principles and aspirations, and the challenges that have hindered their full implementation.

Chapter 2

Unemployment: The Broken Economic Promise

Current Unemployment Rates and Their Impact

South Africa's official unemployment rate was 33.2% in the second quarter of 2025, according to the Quarterly Labour Force Survey (QLFS). This escalating rate is alarming. Decades ago, unemployment was not nearly as severe, and what makes today's crisis even more distressing is that the country is filled with graduates and skilled individuals who remain jobless.

Political parties have long used unemployment as a rallying point in their manifestos. Yet, despite promises made election after election, unemployment has only worsened. South Africa no longer needs empty rhetoric—we need concrete solutions.

One of the most contentious issues is the growing number of undocumented foreign nationals living and working in South Africa. Unlike in other countries, where strict border checks, work permits, and visa requirements regulate access to the job market, South Africa has allowed widespread illegal entry and unregulated employment.

A simple walk past fast-food outlets in Durban demonstrates this reality: dozens of scooters are lined up, most driven by foreign nationals. These jobs could provide relief for unemployed South Africans, yet they are occupied by those who entered the country unlawfully. Critics may argue that South Africans reject low-paying jobs, but this only raises a deeper question—why are we normalizing the exploitation of any worker?

The ripple effects are far-reaching. Hiring illegal immigrants means fewer registered citizens are employed, which in turn drives poverty and crime. Unregistered individuals are difficult to trace if they commit crimes, compounding insecurity. Unemployment, therefore, not only robs families of breadwinners; it also fuels drug dealing, prostitution, human trafficking, and broken households as people struggle to survive.

Instead of addressing unemployment with urgency, the government has failed dismally. Posts are sold, nepotism is rampant, and children of politicians secure opportunities while millions remain excluded. Even at the highest levels, parliament often redeploy ministers from one portfolio to another—sometimes recycling officials involved in corruption scandals. This recycling of leadership has produced stagnation and hopelessness, leaving citizens to wonder where the country is truly headed.

The Failure of Economic Policies to Create Jobs

South Africa's economy is overly reliant on mining and finance, which generate wealth but fail to create large-scale employment. A shortage of advanced qualifications exacerbates the problem: many South Africans stop at diplomas or degrees due to funding shortages, while foreigners with master's and PhDs often secure highly skilled jobs.

At the same time, economic strategies frequently ignore the informal sector, which supports millions of livelihoods. Market traders in KwaZulu-Natal, for instance, have worked for decades without support or opportunities for growth. With proper assistance, they could expand and employ more people. Overlooking this sector is a missed opportunity.

Policy frameworks have also been disastrous. The National Development Plan (2012) promised to reduce unemployment to 14% by 2020 and 6% by 2030. Instead, disorganization, corruption, and empty promises derailed progress. Presidential employment initiatives created only temporary jobs, failing to address the long-term issue of unemployment. Frequent policy changes, looting of funds, and corruption have driven away investment.

Labour laws protect those already employed but discourage firms from hiring new workers due to high costs and risks. Weak education and inadequate job training often mean that young people lack employable skills, despite the presence of vocational institutions. Entrepreneurship is seldom encouraged, and black South Africans, in particular, have not been adequately prepared for business ownership.

The taxi industry exemplifies this dysfunction. Taxis move more than 60% of commuters daily but remain poorly regulated, unsafe, and prone to violent conflict. Government oversight is minimal, subsidies favour buses and trains over taxis, and repeated promises of formalisation never materialise. This sector, like so many others, is left in chaos while citizens suffer.

Franklin D. Roosevelt's New Deal Lessons

When Franklin D. Roosevelt became U.S. President in 1933, America was in the depths of the Great Depression. One in four Americans was unemployed, banks were collapsing, and public confidence was shattered. Roosevelt responded with the New Deal—a bold restructuring of the government's role in the economy.

The New Deal was organized into the "3 Rs":

- **Relief** – direct aid for the unemployed through programs like the Civilian Conservation Corps (CCC).

- **Recovery** – reviving the economy via public works programs such as the Works Progress Administration (WPA).

- **Reform** – systemic changes such as banking regulation and Social Security to prevent future crises.

Positive Outcomes: Millions of jobs were created, infrastructure was built that still stands today, and public confidence was restored.

Drawbacks: Critics argued that some programs created dependency, government debt grew, and unemployment remained high until World War II. Moreover, benefits were uneven—African Americans and women often remained excluded.

Improving on the New Deal for South Africa

South Africa can draw inspiration from the New Deal but must adapt it wisely:

1. **Preventing Dependency** – Pair relief programs with training and mentorship to ensure people transition into sustainable employment.

2. **Balanced Government Spending** – Fund programs responsibly, with strong oversight to prevent debt and corruption.

3. **Inclusive Participation** – Prioritize youth, women, and marginalized communities.

4. **Private-Public Partnerships** – Share resources and risks between government, businesses, and communities.

5. **Constructive Labour Relations** – Unlike South Africa today, Roosevelt balanced union demands with economic stability. Mismanaged strikes here cripple industries, while FDR's reforms mediated disputes. South Africa must build frameworks that protect workers' rights without paralyzing companies.

By refining these lessons, South Africa could pursue large-scale reforms that create real work opportunities. As the Freedom Charter declared: *"There shall be work and security."* This promise will only be fulfilled if we move beyond empty rhetoric toward bold, inclusive, and carefully managed reforms.

The Role of Trade Unions

As of March 2025, there are 204 registered trade unions in South Africa.

Historical Role

According to historical records, early trade unions were often for whites only, with organizations like the South African Confederation of Labour (SACoL) favouring employment policies based on racial discrimination. They also often excluded women. Mary Fitzgerald is considered the first female South African trade unionist, having led numerous strikes and sit-ins before 1911.

The first trade union to organize black workers was the Industrial Workers of Africa (IWA), formed in September 1917 by the revolutionary syndicalist International Socialist League (ISL). The IWA merged into the Industrial and Commercial Workers' Union of Africa (ICU), formed in 1919. Initially, the ICU organized black and coloured dockworkers in Cape Town, before expanding to include rural farm workers, domestic and factory workers, dockworkers, teachers, and retailers.

Trade unions, especially those under the Congress of South African Trade Unions (COSATU), were at the forefront of the fight against apartheid, mobilizing workers for democracy and social justice. COSATU formed part of the Tripartite Alliance with the African National Congress (ANC) and the South African Communist Party (SACP), ensuring that workers' issues were tied to national liberation and post-apartheid policymaking.

Unions negotiated wages, working conditions, benefits, and job security at a collective level, making it easier for employees who would otherwise struggle to negotiate individually. They also represented workers in disputes, strikes, and forums such as the Commission for Conciliation, Mediation, and Arbitration (CCMA). They lobbied for pro-worker laws, such as the Labour Relations Act (1995) and the Basic Conditions of Employment Act (1997), and pushed for fair wages, healthcare, pensions, and housing allowances.

Beyond workplace advocacy, trade unions expanded their mandate to broader social justice issues, including inequality, poverty, and public service delivery. *Their ability to mobilize millions of members gave them strong political influence.*

However, today, many unions no longer focus on the genuine needs of workers. They have become political battlegrounds, prioritizing party interests over worker welfare.

Unequal Pay and Underemployment

One of the many failures of government has been the lack of action on wage inequality. Black South Africans often earn less than their white counterparts, even when doing the same jobs. On average, whites earn the most, followed by Asians/Indians, then Coloureds, with black workers earning the least.

Research also shows disparities along gender lines: men earn more than women in most industries. These wage gaps fuel ongoing inequality, since income determines a person's lifestyle and opportunities.

Many black households survive on minimum wage. For example, in a family of five with one breadwinner earning R5,000, basic expenses such as bread (R20 a loaf, requiring at least two loaves a day), electricity, water, transport, and toiletries quickly consume the entire salary. Bread alone can account for nearly a quarter of a person's monthly income.

The apartheid system entrenched white privilege, ensuring that remuneration was unequal and dignity was denied to black workers. Even today, qualified black graduates often remain in entry-level jobs, while less qualified white counterparts hold managerial positions with higher pay.

Although the Promotion of Equality and Prevention of Unfair Discrimination Act (2000) was designed to prevent wage discrimination, the problem persists. Labour inspections frequently overlook it, and the government has failed to enforce compliance effectively.

This reality is deeply discouraging. More than 30 years into democracy, many South Africans still experience systemic wage inequality and underemployment. Employers and the labour department must do better to redress these injustices.

Trade Unions, Strikes, and Mismanagement

Trade unions were once a cornerstone of the struggle against apartheid and remain vital for protecting workers' rights. Yet, in modern South Africa, their influence sometimes worsens unemployment.

Strikes—while legitimate—often paralyze industries, disrupt supply chains, and cause companies to collapse. When labour disputes are mishandled, businesses lose resources, retrench workers, or shut down altogether. In struggling sectors like mining and manufacturing, unrealistic demands can accelerate job losses or deter investors. Poor government mediation compounds the problem.

This reality underscores the urgent need for responsible union leadership and effective dispute resolution—ensuring workers' dignity is preserved while keeping industries alive. Without this balance, the very structures designed to protect workers will continue to contribute to the unemployment crisis.

Chapter 3

Education for All

Challenges in Access and Quality of Education

Education remains the pivotal topic of debate in South Africa. Why? Because of the inequality that has persisted since apartheid. Examining South Africa's history, one cannot help but discuss the role of various education systems that played a significant part in shaping protests across the country.

Remembering the Youth of 1976—the Soweto Uprising—when approximately 20,000 black students marched against the oppressive Afrikaans Medium Decree that forced them to learn in a language they barely spoke. What began as a peaceful student protest turned tragic when police fired on the unarmed children, killing hundreds. Thanks to the bravery of Hector Pieterson and many others, that uprising still echoes today. Let us look at what Bantu Education entailed:

Black people were limited to:

- Manual labour and jobs requiring little skill: mine work, domestic work, factory work, farm work, and other manual labour.

- Clerical and administrative jobs: many families recall relatives who worked as clerks, drivers, post deliverers, or shop assistants. These were usually low-paying jobs.

- Teaching: Black South Africans could become teachers, but only within the "Bantu Education" system of schools.

- Nursing: Allowed only at a basic level, restricted to black hospitals, and under strict supervision.

Professions they were excluded from: Black South Africans were largely prohibited from becoming engineers, doctors, lawyers, accountants, scientists, architects, or holding senior management positions. Some were allowed to study law or similar professions to represent black people, but always under tight restrictions and oversight. Universities were segregated, and most higher education fields were closed to black students unless the Minister of Education granted special permission.

- **Before 1959**: With ministerial consent, black students could study at "whites only" universities such as Wits, UCT, or Stellenbosch.

- **After 1959**, the University Education Act officially barred black students from these universities, except by ministerial permission. The state built new universities for specific black ethnic groups.

Universities designated for Black South Africans:

- **University of Fort Hare** (Eastern Cape) – for Xhosa-speaking students (though initially open to all tribes; even leaders like Robert Mugabe studied there).

- **University of Zululand** (KwaZulu-Natal) – for Zulu students.

- **University of the North** (Turfloop, Limpopo) – for Sotho, Venda, Tsonga, and Pedi students.

- **University of the Western Cape** (UWC) – for Coloured students.

- **University of Durban-Westville** (UDW) – for Indian students.

- **University of Venda** – for students from the Venda-speaking community.

- **University of Transkei** (UNITRA) – for Xhosa students in Transkei.

- **University of Bophuthatswana** (UNIBO) – for Tswana-speaking students.

- **Medunsa** (Medical University of South Africa) – established in 1976 to train black doctors.

While these institutions did not explicitly ban other racial groups, they were clearly designed with tribal and racial segregation in mind. Nonetheless, they produced remarkable leaders, judges, and politicians of high calibre.

The apartheid government, particularly through H.F. Verwoerd, openly stated that the purpose of "black education" was to prevent black South Africans from competing with whites in skilled professions.

Key points of Bantu Education:

- **Poor quality education**: Curriculum designed to prepare black learners for manual labour, not professional careers.

- **Racial exclusion**: White schools received far more funding and resources.

- **Central control**: Black education was placed under the Department of Native Affairs, headed by Verwoerd, who declared that black learners should not be taught to aspire beyond their "station" in life.

Effects of Bantu Education:

- Created deep educational inequalities that persist today.

- Sparked protests and uprisings, most notably the 1976 Soweto Uprising, where students resisted Afrikaans instruction and many lost their lives.

- Denied black South Africans access to economic development.

Bantu Education was more than an education policy—it was a weapon of apartheid designed to impose inequality. Its legacy has carried on for generations and will take many more years to undo.

The Current Education System

Although the country has abolished Bantu Education, the current system is not significantly better. The minimum pass requirements in high school leave learners underprepared for higher education, where a 50% pass per subject is required.

Matric pass categories:

1. **Higher Certificate**

   o At least 40% in Home Language.

   o At least 40% in two other subjects.

   o At least 30% in three other subjects.

   o May fail one subject with a grade below 30% and still pass overall.

- Qualifies for entry into many certificate courses at colleges.

2. **Diploma Pass**

   - At least 40% in four subjects (including Home Language).

   - At least 30% in three other subjects.

   - Qualifies for entry into diploma courses at universities or TVET colleges.

3. **Bachelor's Pass**

   - At least 40% in Home Language.

   - At least 50% in four designated subjects (required for university).

   - At least 30% in two other subjects.

   - Qualifies for entry into degree study at universities.

While this policy inflates pass rates, it dilutes the quality of education. Students often arrive at university unprepared, leading to high failure rates, frustration, and wasted resources.

The Case for STEM Prioritization

Studies by UNESCO and the OECD reveal that nations investing in STEM (Science, Technology, Engineering, Mathematics) education achieve higher levels of innovation, employment, and global competitiveness. South Africa's lowered education standards undermine this potential.

Government should establish specialized centres for mathematics and science tutoring—after school and on weekends—with labs, mentors, and structured support. This would help address bottlenecks in critical subjects and open doors for learners into careers that can advance national development.

Case Study: The Soviet Union's Rise Through Education and Industrial Policy

After the 1917 Russian Revolution, the Soviet Union was a poor, rural, and largely illiterate nation. Yet, by the mid-20th century, it had become a superpower, competing with the U.S. in science, technology, and military strength.

Key elements of Soviet success:

1. **Mass Literacy Campaigns**: Within two decades, literacy became nearly universal.

2. **STEM Prioritisation**: Heavy investment in engineering, mathematics, and science produced millions of specialists. Scientists and engineers were celebrated as heroes.

3. **Linking Education to Industry**: Education fed directly into industrialization, powering factories, infrastructure, and later the space program.

4. **Results**: By the 1950s, the USSR had transformed into an industrial giant, launching Sputnik in 1957 and producing Nobel Prize winners.

5. **Criticisms**: The system was rigid, prioritised state goals over individual freedoms, and suppressed the arts and humanities.

Lessons for South Africa:

- STEM investment drives growth.
- Technical and vocational education (TVETs) should be elevated as prestigious, not fallback options.
- State vision must be deliberate and well-coordinated.
- Balance is necessary—education reform must support critical thinking, entrepreneurship, and democratic values alongside STEM.

The Struggle for Free Quality Education

One of the most debated issues in South Africa is whether free higher education is possible.

The #FeesMustFall movement in 2015 highlighted the crisis:

- Escalating tuition excluded students from poor backgrounds.
- Government subsidies had declined, forcing universities to rely heavily on student fees.

- Protests quickly spread nationwide, uniting students across racial and class divides.

Government response:

- In October 2015, President Jacob Zuma announced a 0% fee increase for the 2016 academic year.

- A commission of inquiry followed, leading to the phased introduction of free higher education for poor and working-class families from 2018 onwards, administered through the National Student Financial Aid Scheme (NSFAS).

Who qualifies:

- Students from households earning under R350,000 annually.

- Students with disabilities qualify if the household income is under R600,000.

- NSFAS covers tuition, registration, accommodation, meals, transport, and study materials.

Limitations:

- Middle-income families (the "missing middle") are excluded and still struggle.

- Corruption, delays, and mismanagement persist as ongoing issues for NSFAS.

Despite its challenges, NSFAS remains one of the most impactful interventions for access to higher education in democratic South Africa.

The Right to Education in the Freedom Charter

Section 29 of the Constitution enshrines the right to basic education, and the Freedom Charter envisioned equal access to higher education, technical training, and professional development for all, regardless of wealth or race.

Recent reforms, such as the Basic Education Laws Amendment (BELA) Act of 2024, sought to improve access and regulation. Key points included:

- Compulsory Grade R attendance.

- Prohibition of school exclusion for lack of identity documents.

- Ban on corporal punishment.

- Regular review of school admission policies.

- Expansion of language options when necessary.

While these reforms aim for inclusivity, they have stirred controversy—particularly regarding undocumented learners, as many South Africans fear this compromises resources for citizens.

The Impact of Student Protests and Movements

Student protests—whether over fees, funding, or management—have frequently disrupted educational calendars, damaged infrastructure, and compromised academic outcomes. Learners under pressure to catch up focus on memorization rather than deep learning, producing graduates who struggle to compete globally or start businesses.

While protests highlight real injustices, they also strain resources. Repairing damaged property diverts money from improvements such as modern classrooms or technology.

The legacy of apartheid education remains a burden. Unless bold reforms are undertaken—prioritizing STEM, addressing inequality, curbing corruption, and balancing inclusivity with sustainability—South Africa will remain trapped in cycles of frustration and lost potential.

Chapter 4

Land Reform: The Controversy of

Expropriation Without Compensation

L and reform in South Africa is one of the most pivotal and controversial socio-economic and political issues since the end of apartheid. Its main focus is correcting the historical injustices of land dispossession and ensuring agricultural productivity and economic stability. But how can this be achieved if, after so many years, nothing has been done yet, only conversations that amount to nothing, and how is this going to be implemented in a manner that will not jeopardise a system that is already in place?

Historical Context of Land Dispossession

- The 1913 Natives Land Act and the 1936 Native Trust and Land Act restricted Black South Africans to roughly 13 percent of the country's land. The white minority retained control over most of the fertile, arable land, creating deep economic inequality that still shapes South Africa's landscape today. The government tried to take back some of the land, but it came with a lot of challenges, some were the following:

- Limited budget, our country constantly discusses its limited budget; there is nothing new there. Money would rather be spent on things that don't really matter than allocated to places where it will have a long-term impact. The issue of land is a huge concern, with many people still complaining about the amount of land that was taken away from them without compensation, we all know how debatable this is, with many people believing that land was sold fairly and others believing that people were forcefully removed, this is the reason why townships were started, in order to ensure that black people move from the places that white people chose for themselves, at the same time they couldn't place black people too far because they still needed them for work. That's why the apartheid government built the four-roomed houses to keep black people around, but not close enough to be a "nuisance" to them. This disparity is still visible even today. Today, that divide still shows. Suburbs generally enjoy uninterrupted services such as running water and electricity, while many neighbouring townships face frequent shortages and infrastructure failures. The contrast mirrors the economic gap between rate-paying and state-dependent communities.

- In the past, communities such as Soweto paid little or nothing for municipal services. Introducing a culture of payment later has been met with resistance—people ask, *"Why now?"* This reveals how difficult it is to shift expectations once dependence on free services becomes entrenched. As the proverb reminds us, *"Don't give a man fish; teach him how to fish."* Once people become accustomed to receiving, it becomes painful when they are asked to provide for themselves again. Over time, we have been conditioned to see the government as our saviour. Many citizens no longer build their own homes but wait for RDP housing to arrive.

- After land had been returned to its rightful owners, many farms failed due to a lack of training and resources. This raises a question about how this will work if we are going to take farms from people who know how to farm and are supplying food all over the country and overseas, thereby increasing the country's GDP and socio-economic development. It is risky to fight a system that works in the name of correcting history. Yes, many people require land, but taking land from people who are working the land to give it to people that will still need government support and a lot of training, and one must remember, farming does not just include ploughing and sowing, it requires plant and machinery, fuel, electricity, workers, security, and many other things that come with the farmwork. This is a sensitive subject, and not only is it sensitive, but it also has serious consequences when not handled with care.

Without getting emotional about it, let us examine the issue of land with a realistic perspective. After land has been taken from farmers, what are we going to do with it? Build houses? Or give it to the people to "see" what they can do with it, the repercussions of that far outweighs the benefits, or maybe we can distribute the land nonetheless. The sense of ownership runs deep: even if one cannot use the land as effectively as its current occupant, the emotional truth remains— *"It is still mine."* Not to downplay the gravity of land reform, but to prevent future repercussions, every transfer must guarantee that the land will be used productively. Idle land helps no one.

One of the main issues that stalls the entire process is the people entitled to the land; many individuals will fight for the same land, which makes it difficult for the rightful owners to be awarded the land. But since the land act is such a sensitive issue that requires a lot of scrutiny and a lot of analytics, we will put it to rest here, I wouldn't want to expand on it, because my family too had to surrender land, but when we look at what has been achieved through the land that we would claim as ours, we look at it with pride and cheer. South Africa needs more than land; we need jobs, and we need to be reconditioned to think in a certain way. I often watch people in Hostels in Johannesburg who have been living there for 20+ years, still complaining about how the government promised them houses, but they are still waiting.

Let us be more realistic. In Johannesburg, I often see people who have lived in hostels for over twenty years still waiting for the government to fulfil housing promises. It's a painful picture of dependence and delayed hope.

Do you remember back in Cape Town Khayelitsha back in 2009, when toilets were given to people but they were just toilets with no walls, and people were complaining about their dignity, the DA maintained that the community must close the walls, this shows that we are fully dependant on the government for everything, yes, because we were conditioned that way, but what can we do as the new South Africa to ensure that we are not people who rely on the government for everything, we need to ensure that we stand together as a community to do our own things, and not wait for the government because it seems like we will wait for a very long time.

We must try and prove the likes of JBM Hertzog wrong, he said, "a black person is a permanent child". This was meant to cripple black people and make them fully dependent, but we are better than that, we were not made to be slaves and to wait for someone to build houses for us.

Many years ago, in the rural areas people used to build mud houses, and those structures used to stand the test of times, and we used to plant our own crops and circulate our own food in the communities, but if you go around many rural areas, you will find very few homes who have green gardens, because we have been conditioned that the government is our messiah. One of the reasons this book is written is to realise our full potential, to take us back into time to think about the times where we didn't rely on anyone to do anything for us, where our forefathers used to walk miles to school just to get education, this seems like going back in time, I know people need development, they want to see progress. However, remember that progress comes at a cost. We may have the freedom to vote and hope that whoever we have voted for will provide us with everything we need, but life is not like that. Life requires you to work hard for what you have.

The money that the government uses comes from taxpayers, and taxpayers are the same people who wake up every day to face hard working conditions, wake up every day, hot or cold, to ensure that food is on the table, and over and above that, a portion of their earnings goes to the government to ensure that the well-being of everyone is improved. This is not to say that some people will sit and wait for service delivery, while others must indirectly facilitate it. We must work together as a community to ensure that everyone works hard for what they have. Before we protest and cause riots, we need to be realistic and ensure that we know how the government works and where the money for all the service delivery comes from.

- Corruption and elite capture -land sometimes benefits connected individuals rather than poor communities.

- Legal battles over restitution claims, the ongoing battle about the rightful owners, drag the process, and rightfully so, because this will create unnecessary disputes if the wrong people are awarded land.

Land Issue: An Ancient Problem

The issue of land is one of the hardest conversations to have; it always leaves people emotional. If we look at history, we need to identify the root cause of what happened during the land trade.

The information we have might be inaccurate because, like the African proverb says, "until the lion learns how to write, every story will glorify the hunter.

We were given land by God, from time immemorial, and the demarcation of land determined who owned what part of the land and which tribe belonged to which part.

The fundamental thing to note above all this is that we all found land here. Maybe God should have done the demarcation himself; we wouldn't have the dilemma we have today. Or maybe he did give us land, but we decided to move beyond our bounds.

In economics, land is a very important component; there are four components that we can mention: Land, Labour, Capital and Entrepreneurship. The four factors of production are pivotal in every economy; if you have one without the other, it can be quite difficult.

We must look at how land was transferred to the whites, because the issue of Land started after the arrival of the whites. I believe that we lived harmoniously in our country before the arrival of the whites. Again, this book is not to create any anger towards any racial groups, but in order for us to rewrite history, we must write it as it is; we shouldn't sugarcoat anything. Apartheid was no secret, and we are still nursing the scars to this day. Again, the story of the lion, we only know a certain side of history, but we don't know the other side of history; we can only assume what happened based on current events and conviction.

Before we dissect the issue of land, it is essential to understand exactly what we are referring to when discussing land expropriation. When you drive around anywhere, you will see vast land that is unoccupied. Then, you will ask yourself, what are they talking about when they say we don't have land?

The issue of land also takes us back to colonization, which is the main culprit of land grabs, and it is important to know who colonised us. We will focus on South Africa in particular.

It will be a stretch if we try to dissect the full history in its entirety, but by focusing on the world, we will reference it here and there.

Anglo-Boer War

They say when two elephants fight, it is the grass that suffers. Imagine two colonizers coming to a peaceful country to fight; it is unheard of, but this is South Africa's reality. Although it may have occurred in other countries, our focus will remain here. Let us look at what the war was for and for what.

The Anglo-Boer War (1899–1902) was a conflict between the British Empire and two independent Boer republics: Transvaal and the Orange Free State. It was one of the most memorable wars in South African history because it remodelled the country economically and socially.

Causes of the War

1. Control of Gold and Diamonds

   o The discovery of diamonds (1867) and gold (1886) made South Africa the focal point, and it was these two "allies" who decided to fight amongst themselves. Funny enough, at that point, I doubt anyone thought of the "natives".

○ Britain sought full control over the region, while the Boer republics aimed to maintain their independence.

For context, the Boers were descendants of Dutch settlers and some German and French Huguenot immigrants who arrived at the Cape of Good Hope during the 1600s and 1700s, when the region was under Dutch control. The word *Boer* means "farmer" in Dutch/Afrikaans, reflecting their identity as rural settlers. So, now that we understand who they were/are, they came here and fought for the minerals, which belonged to South Africans in the first place. Yes, the natives didn't even know anything about the minerals, but the least that these parties could have done was to ensure that whoever owned the land they "discovered" the minerals on was well compensated. They may have been compensated, but we will not dwell on who is the rightful owner or why things happened the way they did. The truth is, we are focusing mainly on post-apartheid. However, the primary purpose of history is to look back and see where everything originated. At this point, this was also the genesis of many of our problems; wealth was distributed amongst a group of minority races, and the rightful landowners were left desolate and begging for attention.

One cannot help but wonder why God allowed black people to always fall at the bottom of the food chain, Professor P. L. O. Lumumba said in one of his quotes, "*Are we serving a lesser God?*"

The reason why the land issue brings tears into our eyes is because of the impact it has had in our country; it left the country lopsided, and this is one of the things that are too hard to rewrite and correct, talk about punching where it hurts. Hence, I tread carefully when discussing the issue of land, because if not addressed appropriately, it might leave a bitter taste in the mouth.

Although the Anglo-Boer War is often portrayed as a struggle between the British Empire and the Afrikaners, the greatest losers were Black South Africans. They were drawn into the conflict but denied recognition and rights after it ended.

My advice is that we need a government that will eventually address this issue, not tiptoe around it, cause a stir, and leave it hanging. We chant the song, "*thina sizwe esimnyama sikhalela izwe lethu elathathwa abamhlophe, mabawuyeke umhlaba wethu*", how long are we going to sing without addressing the issue? Or must we just let it go and try other means? What is the solution, fellow South Africans? Please, let us stop endless discussions and take action. Alternatively, let us consider Plan B, as we wait for the land to be returned to its rightful owners is like waiting for rain in a desert - it is fruitless and disappointing.

Public Sentiment and Political Ramifications

As mentioned earlier, the issue of land has created inequality.

Land reform has moved slowly since 1994, with the government often criticised for being inefficient and failing to benefit poor rural communities. In 2017, the ANC adopted the principle of expropriation of land without compensation (EWC) as a tool to accelerate land reform.

Many Black South Africans see EWC as a corrective measure that should have been taken a long time ago, stating that land was taken violently in the past and must now be returned without payment. Some people believe that it will address historical dispossession, reduce inequality, and restore dignity. Movements like the EFF (Economic Freedom Fighters) gained popularity by being at the forefront of this movement. They strongly believe that this will correct history, and, in my opinion, I salute the EFF for having such a strong stand against the injustices of the past. But we are at a standstill because we need this to be actioned accordingly without causing another unprecedented South African war.

Concerns

- Some communities, particularly farmers and property owners, fear that EWC could disturb food security, the economy, and we might lose investor confidence. As it is, we had President Trump, who tweeted that there is white genocide in South Africa, which is targeting white farmers; this caused quite a stir in our country to the extent that our president and his entourage had to fly to the United States to correct this narrative. 49 "Farmers" went to America when President Trump offered refugee status for the alleged threatened white farmers who were under serious "threat". It didn't help us that we already have a pending case of expropriation of land without compensation, you know what they say, rumours always spread like wildfire, and if they have spread long enough, they become truth. It was a nightmare to defend South Africa at that point, and it didn't help that we have a song, "*dubul'ibhunu*", which loosely translates kill the Boer, kill the farmer.

The origin of the song comes from the apartheid era, when Black South Africans were oppressed under white minority rule. It was sung by activists, especially Umkhonto we Sizwe (MK), the armed wing of the African National Congress (ANC). The lyrics were not meant literally to call for killing farmers but rather used to express resistance against the apartheid regime, which was strongly associated with the white Afrikaners.

- So, with all the above being mentioned, many surveys show that most South Africans support land reform, but some are against the expropriation of land, with obvious fear of war. Many prefer redistribution through government purchase of land and restitution programmes.

- Critics fear risks of repeating the Zimbabwean land confiscations of the 2000s, which led to agricultural collapse. Zimbabwe has vast land that belongs to the people, but poverty has escalated because the land is no longer utilised for agricultural purposes. Land is just sitting, collecting dust. We don't want to face the same realities in South Africa, where many people leave their home country in search of greener pastures elsewhere. The whole world applauded Zimbabwe for regaining its land, but what is the use of having vast unworked land and poverty? Before we make any kind of movement, we need to calculate the risks involved.

- Middle-class South Africans of all racial groups panic about the possible loss of property rights and economic recession if EWC is not carefully managed. There is frustration with the government's failure to deliver meaningful land reform since 1994, which has led to more radical demands.

Bantu Land Act

The Bantu Land Act of 1913, also called the Natives Land Act, was one of the most devastating pieces of legislation in South African history. It institutionalised land dispossession for Black South Africans. Under this Act, only about 7% of South Africa's land was allocated for natives, while the rest was reserved for whites. Later amendments increased this figure to around 13%, but the majority of rich and arable land was exclusively reserved for whites.

Purpose

The main aim of the Act was to regulate land ownership, but in reality, it established racial segregation and poverty. Black people were prohibited from owning land outside the designated "reserves." Families lost ancestral lands, cattle farming collapsed, and rural poverty deepened.

Government Failure

The Act reflects an intense failure of government on compound levels:

1. **Failure to Protect Citizens**

    Instead of defending the rights of all South Africans, the government actively discriminated against the majority population. By endorsing laws that stripped Black people of land, they stripped them of their basic human rights.

2. **Failure to Promote Economic Development**

    The Land Act destroyed the agricultural independence of millions. It created a cycle of poverty that is still prevalent today, as descendants of dispossessed communities remain with no land and are crowded in underdeveloped rural "homelands." Even after the establishment of democracy in 1994, the legacy of this injustice persists.

The issue of land is more than just economic development if it hinders traditional governance and identity, as people are uprooted from their ancestral land and placed in locations that compromise their culture. This is because people in these locations are often perceived as having no culture, mainly due to a lack of identity. Their peace was disturbed, and this resulted in a new adopted way of life. When the Land Act was introduced, it removed people from their homelands where they practised their spirituality and culture, but the arrival of the whites and missionaries ensured that all that was not possible. People were introduced to a new way of life and were required to worship God in a specific manner. It is a nightmare when you think about it. Bantu people are spiritual beings naturally, but now black people are lost; some of them don't know if they are coming or going.

How can we not blame the government for such failures?

For centuries, African communities lived on and cultivated land that had been passed down through generations. The Bantu Land Act (1913) upset this continuity by making it illegal for black Africans to own land in certain areas. Families who had buried their ancestors on certain lands were suddenly classified as "squatters" on their own soil. The loss was not only economic but deeply cultural and spiritual, it broke the bond between people and their heritage.

Continuity Between the 1913 Land Act and Post-1994 Land Reform Failures

Legacy of the 1913 Act

When democracy arrived in 1994, land inequality was one of the blatant legacies of apartheid: whites, who made up less than 10% of the population, owned more than 80% of the land, while the Black majority remained largely landless.

Promise of Land Reform Post 1994

The new democratic government acknowledged this injustice and promised land reform under three pillars:

1. **Restitution** – giving land back to those dispossessed.

2. **Redistribution** – providing land to the landless.

3. **Tenure reform** – Procuring rights for those living on land without ownership.

The target was to redistribute 30% of commercial farmland to Black South Africans by 2014.

The Failure of Implementation

After 31 years, progress has been awfully slow:

- By 2018, less than 10% of land had been transferred, far below the target.

- Many restitution claims remain unresolved, leaving communities to wait for decades for justice.

- Redistributed farms often lack government support, leading to cases where land becomes underutilised, as we mentioned with the issue of Zimbabwe, where land was taken over and not utilised. The reality is appropriated land still requires government support and funds injections, which leads to more corruption and looting of funds, and the government lacks the capacity to ensure that all the farms that are appropriated are used for farming and the amount of money to ensure that has to be injected to see if this is possible will be too much.

- Corruption means that land often goes to politically connected individuals, not to the rural poor who lost it in 1913.

While the 1913 Act physically expelled people from their ancestral land, many still cannot return or secure land due to the slow pace of restitution. Millions remain "uprooted". Rural communities remain overcrowded in former homelands, a direct echo of the reality created by the Land Act.

The post-1994 government has failed to rectify this injustice quickly enough. Both failures leave the majority without land, keeping inequality at the centre of South African society.

The Bantu Land Act of 1913 was not just a past injustice; it created a wound that the democratic government has promised to heal, but has struggled to do so. Land reform has become a symbol of the ongoing failure of the South African government to protect its citizens, dating back to 1913, and today, to deliver justice despite having the political mandate to do so.

At its core, land reform is not just about ownership—it is about food security. Arable land must remain dedicated to agriculture. If redistributed land lies unused, the nation risks hunger and economic collapse.

South Africa must avoid the mistake of converting fertile farmland into housing projects at the expense of food production. Redistribution must be conditional: land given for farming must be used for farming, with government support for training, irrigation, credit, and machinery.

Learning from Failures of Other SADC Countries

Zimbabwe: The Consequences of Farm Nationalization

Introduction

The experiences of neighbouring countries in the Southern African Development Community (SADC) provide valuable lessons for South Africa in its mission to realize the promises of the *Freedom Charter*. Zimbabwe offers a cautionary story. The government's decision in the early 2000s to pursue a major land reform programme, commonly referred to as farm nationalisation or the "Fast Track Land Reform Programme" (FTLRP), had serious political, social, and economic consequences. While the policy was framed as an effort to correct historical injustices caused by colonial land dispossession, its implementation undermined agricultural production, collapsed investor confidence, and deepened economic destitution.

Historical Background

At independence in 1980, Zimbabwe inherited an unequal land distribution system where white commercial farmers owned the majority of arable land. Initial land reform policies were slow, negotiated, and market-driven under the Lancaster House Agreement. By the late 1990s, however, mounting social pressure and political opposition led the government to adopt a more aggressive approach. In 2000, the state sanctioned the occupation and redistribution of white-owned commercial farms, often through violent seizures rather than structured policy implementation (Moyo, 2011).

Consequences of Farm Nationalization

1. Agricultural Collapse

Zimbabwe was once considered the "breadbasket of Africa," producing surplus maize, tobacco, and other crops. The sudden displacement of experienced commercial farmers, without adequate support for new farmers, caused a dramatic decline in production. Between 2000 and 2009, maize output decreased by nearly 70%, while tobacco production declined by more than 50% (Richardson, 2005). This collapse left the country dependent on food imports and aid. This is the same trajectory that South Africa is yet to face if we continue to pursue expropriation of land from people who are utilising it for agricultural purposes. We cannot rewrite history, as much as we want the world to go back to its former glory, but the problem is that we need more than just repossession of land; we need to be financially ready to take over, and we need the right education to ensure sustainability.

Agriculture requires skills that are learnt over a period, not just textbook knowledge. We need to know what grows and in what season, what works and what doesn't work. We think it's just correcting the injustices of the past, but the truth is, it is reconstructing what works, to go back to square one. And it will not be easy; it will not be without challenges. We must brace ourselves for a new economic downturn that will take years to recover from.

2. Economic Decline

The land seizures led to a loss of investor confidence and resulted in international sanctions. We know what happened in 2025, with America activating sanctions, which led to many countries suffering because sanctions are political wars and responses. We have giant countries that are holding us by their teeth, and if they release, we are bound to collapse. We are all connected to each other; we mustn't let our emotions forget about the looming trade wars. Farmers create connections and allies over time, and when they relinquish their farms, they also sever all their contacts. As a result, we are left with pieces of land that will be useless. Zimbabwe's GDP shrank by more than 40% between 2000 and 2008 (World Bank, 2010). Hyperinflation reached unprecedented levels, peaking at 231 million percent in 2008, effectively destroying the local currency and wiping out savings. The economic collapse led to widespread unemployment and a mass exodus of skilled workers. Today, we see many Zimbabweans fleeing their country. If the expropriation of land was amazing, then why do we see a mass exodus from these countries?

3. Food Insecurity and Humanitarian Crisis

The decline in agriculture directly translated into food shortages. Millions of Zimbabweans faced hunger, with the UN World Food Programme reporting that by 2008, nearly half the population needed food aid (WFP, 2008). The humanitarian crisis was further aggravated by droughts and weak state capacity to respond effectively.

4. Political Repression and Democratic Backsliding

Farm nationalization was also used as a political tool by the ruling party, ZANU-PF, to consolidate power and suppress opposition. Violent land invasions, intimidation, and human rights abuses became widespread. Today, we see numerous fruitless protests, and what lessons are we learning from these countries if we are heading in the same direction as them? We are not saying we must let injustices continue just because we are scared of what might happen, but if something works, then why change it for something that you don't even know if it will work?

Lessons for South Africa

Zimbabwe's experience highlights several lessons relevant to South Africa's land reform debate:

1. **Policy Implementation Matters** – Redressing historical land dispossession is legitimate, but poorly planned and politically manipulated implementation can destroy productive capacity.

2. **Balancing Justice with Stability** – Equitable redistribution must be managed in a way that preserves food security and economic stability.

3. **Avoiding Politicization** – Land reform must not be used as a political weapon to establish ruling parties

but as a developmental strategy benefiting society as a whole. In South Africa, this appears to be a tactic used to encourage people to vote for certain parties; it shouldn't be the case. Land reform must be a tool to equalise the economy, to ensure that previous injustices are corrected, and, of course, with a permanent plan in place to ensure a smooth transition.

Zimbabwe's land nationalization programme was driven by a just cause, correcting colonial-era land inequalities, but its coercive implementation produced devastating consequences. The collapse of agriculture, economic breakdown, food insecurity, and democratic backsliding highlight the dangers of radical, unstructured reform. For South Africa, the Zimbabwean experience serves as a warning: land reform must be pursued in a way that combines justice with sustainability, equity with productivity, and redress with national development.

Zimbabwe's failed populist-based land reform must serve as a lesson for South Africa on how land reform must be rational, to safe-guard commercial agriculture and focus on boosting sustenance.

In 2016, then-Zimbabwean President Robert Mugabe declared a state of disaster for agriculture, a declaration that called for international donors to provide assistance. This declaration was also a clear indication that land reform had failed.

- **Fiscal and Monetary Mismanagement:**

  Poor and often contradictory government policies led to excessive spending, budget deficits, and the printing of money to fund the government, which directly fuelled inflation.

- **Hyperinflation:**

  The Zimbabwean dollar experienced extreme devaluation, reaching cosmic inflation rates in the late 2000s, making it nearly worthless.

- **Corruption and Mismanagement:**

  Widespread corruption and poor governance hindered efforts to restore confidence. The saddest reality at this point is that our country has reached shocking proportions of corruption, and this is one of the many things that led Zimbabwe to collapse. Corruption became a norm, and those who perpetrate crimes are not punished. The development is not possible because the millions of rands are misdirected. They benefit only a few people.

Zambia: Mineral Nationalization and International Investment

Zambia's experience with mineral nationalization provides another important lesson for South Africa as it navigates debates around economic transformation and state ownership. Copper mining has historically been the backbone of Zambia's economy, contributing over 90% of export earnings during the 1970s (Fraser & Lungu, 2007). However, the decision to nationalize the mines in the early post-independence period had far-reaching economic consequences. While intended to secure sovereignty over resources and redistribute wealth, the policy ultimately led to inefficiency, declining investment, and long-term dependence on foreign aid.

Historical Background

After independence in 1964, Zambia's first president, Kenneth Kaunda, sought to reduce foreign dominance over the economy. By 1970, the government had fully nationalized the copper industry, placing it under state control through the Zambia Consolidated Copper Mines (ZCCM).

Initially, the boom in global copper prices allowed the government to finance social spending, infrastructure development, and expanded public services. However, the global decline in copper prices from the mid-1970s exposed weaknesses in the nationalized system.

Consequences of Mineral Nationalization

Without competition or reinvestment, the state-owned ZCCM became increasingly inefficient. The nationalized system left Zambia heavily reliant on copper revenues. When global copper prices collapsed in the 1970s and 1980s, government revenues plunged.

The inefficiencies of nationalization combined with austerity measures had devastating social impacts. Poverty rates rocketed, social spending declined, and inequality deepened. Communities dependent on mining towns experienced unemployment, deteriorating services, and mass retrenchments.

Lessons for South Africa

Zambia's mineral nationalization offers several key lessons:

1. Nationalization without skilled management, reinvestment, and innovation leads to inefficiency and decline.

2. An economy overly reliant on one resource is vulnerable to price fluctuations. South Africa must diversify beyond mining to achieve sustainable growth.

3. While resource sovereignty is important, maintaining investor confidence is crucial. Policies that scare off investment risk undermine long-term development.

4. Economic restructuring must prioritize social protection to avoid worsening poverty and inequality.

Zambia's mineral nationalization validates the dangers of poorly managed state ownership combined with economic dependence on a single commodity. Although intended to achieve sovereignty and wealth redistribution, the policy ultimately weakened the mining industry, discouraged international investment, and worsened social outcomes. For

South Africa, Zambia's experience shows that resource nationalism must be carefully balanced with efficiency, diversification, and investor confidence if it is to contribute meaningfully to realizing the *Freedom Charter's* vision of shared prosperity. What is the use of having minerals that will not attract any investors? South Africa needs a more strategic approach to doing anything in the name of correcting injustices of the past, especially in a country riddled with crime. Moving on will allow corruption to continue.

Chapter 5

Health Care: Access and Inequality

The Right to Health Care in the Freedom Charter

The chant "*Aluta continua*" (The struggle continues) has never been so true as it is today. Instead of making progress, we seem to be moving backwards; the struggle never seems to end. Government facilities used to work 24/7 because it only made sense because they serve the entire community, most people require to be serviced on weekends because they work during the week, but post-apartheid, this is no longer the case; you have to wait until Monday to get assistance. Outpatient Clinics and Specialist Appointments are usually closed on weekends, with services resuming Monday to Friday during office hours. We have lost the plot, a public servant used to be someone who offered themselves to serve the people, it is a nightmare to wait for the weekend to finish only to be attended you on Monday the following week, facilities are always full and have irritable staff, we have to keep circling back to the apartheid government because even though not everything was perfect during that time, but there were proper structures and processes, which is something that is a myth in this day and age.

Try to visit any government office today, and you will find people who are angry, who do not want to work! I don't know why we still call them public servants; we should just call them government employees, because the lack of urgency and customer care is disheartening. One can't help but wonder if they lack support, or are they earning lower salaries and they have a lot of work, so they feel like they must do the bare minimum because they feel unappreciated? The government needs to look into this because this can't be an ongoing outcry forever. This requires some sort of intervention to change the status quo of government facilities.

Beyond poor attitudes and inefficiency, the structural design of public service hours is itself a failure. Critical facilities, including healthcare, operate largely on a 5-day work week, shutting doors to millions who cannot afford to wait until Monday. Health is not a 5-day need—it is a 7-day human right. Public servants in essential services should be required to work staggered shifts across the entire week to guarantee consistent access. Furthermore, the system of compulsory leave around June and the second half of the year severely undermines service delivery. This "one-size-fits-all" policy results in mass staff shortages, delayed procedures, and worsened inefficiency at a time when services should be constant. A comprehensive overhaul of work-hour policies is essential if government facilities are to meet the promises of the Freedom Charter.

Even if you go to the South African Revenue Services (SARS) office, you will find staff that will tell you that you are wasting their time, they want to service the next person, you call the call centre, and wait for hours for someone to assist, when you finally get through, the line gets cut, and they don't call you back. When you try to do a walk-in at the branches, they tell you that you need to set up an appointment, and when you do set up an appointment, the system tells you that the next available date is in 20 days. This is a facility that is supposed to collect taxes from people, yet the service is just appalling, and they garnish people's accounts, yet the inefficiency there is unmatched.

I will not even begin to mention the service rendered at Home Affairs, our home affairs.

The Department of Home Affairs (DHA) facility is one of the most important government institutions in South Africa because it manages the legal identity, citizenship, and movement of people within and across the country's borders. Its role is important, as it touches the lives of every South African and foreign national, both within and outside the country.

The DHA is important as it facilitates governance; without it, people would struggle to prove their identity, which would prevent them from accessing basic services or exercising their rights as citizens, but over the years, it has proven to be one of the most careless government sectors ever.

Tell me why such an important sector has computer systems that often crash or go offline, leaving entire offices unable to process applications? South Africa has moved slowly compared to other countries in modernising identity document, passport, and visa systems.

Many DHA offices are consistently understaffed, particularly in high-demand areas; frontline staff often experience low morale and a lack of accountability. The result is rude treatment of applicants and mistakes in official records, wrong spellings, missing data, and the list goes on.

There have been numerous reports of officials selling fake IDs, passports, or permits to foreign nationals. This damages our credibility in other countries. As a result, if you hold a South African passport, you undergo considerable scrutiny. Many countries no longer have faith in us. We have foreign nationals who commit crimes using our passports and IDs.

Bribery has become rife, deepening inequality because only those who can afford to pay extra receive faster service.

All this is happening because, even if you can report them, no action will be taken. However, thank goodness for the age of social media, where young people can record wrongdoings and post them on social media. If it goes viral and attracts a lot of attention, then action is taken against that official. But must we all take videos in order to correct this?

The way public servants act on the ground is a mirror image of what is happening at the top. The reason they can't be held accountable is that they are certain there are no structures in place to discipline them accordingly. They work together in solidarity, calling each other comrades, and how dare you report a comrade?

The South African Police Service (SAPS) is no better. Today, you find the police officers behind the counter very chatty, with little or no consideration for the people who are there to report serious crimes. To them, everything is a joke, and again, the show shows zero sense of servantship. We are aware that the unemployment rate is high in our country, but people who have jobs seem to be unconcerned.

The Charter states that: *"A preventative health scheme shall be run by the state; free medical care and hospitalization shall be provided for all, with special care for mothers and young children."*

The Freedom Charter's statement about the right to healthcare was one of the most significant liberation movements to dismantle the injustices faced by poor communities, who had to go to understaffed and unequipped hospitals, while white South Africans enjoyed well-equipped hospitals and access to private doctors. By demanding free medical care, preventive health programmes, and healthy living conditions, it opened healthcare to broader scales of achieving dignity and equality. While South Africa has made significant strides since 1994, the persistence of inequality demonstrates that the Charter's vision remains a challenge.

Many public hospitals lack sufficient numbers of doctors, nurses, and specialists. Staff are overworked, leading to burnout and strikes. Many skilled professionals are leaving the country in search of better pay. Clinics and hospitals in rural areas are often in poor condition, with broken equipment, leaking roofs, and insufficient beds. Ambulance services are limited, and people must travel long distances to access primary healthcare.

To bridge the gap between rural and urban healthcare, the government should invest in polyclinics. These facilities would provide comprehensive primary and preventive healthcare within rural and township communities, sparing patients the need to travel long distances for basic treatment. Crucially, polyclinics would also act as referral hubs, ensuring that patients needing specialised treatment are swiftly transferred to appropriate hospitals.

This model has been successfully implemented in other parts of the world, striking a balance between access and efficiency. Polyclinics can serve as a middle ground between under-resourced rural clinics and overcrowded central hospitals, thereby restoring dignity and accessibility to healthcare in neglected regions.

The public healthcare system requires a serious modification. The government often talks about ensuring the dignity of people, but visit one public hospital today, and you will see the dignity of people dragged into the mud.

One of the biggest failures of government is its inability to ensure that healthcare workers treat people well, as, despite public outcry over unfair treatment, there is no change. Aren't health officials taught about the privacy of patients? But how come you find nurses screaming at the top of their voices, "those who are collecting ARVs, come this side!". Where is the dignity that the Freedom Charter wanted to achieve? This never seems to end; instead, it is escalating. It is frightening to know that many people end up not going to the hospitals and clinics to collect their medication because of the fear of being bullied by nurses. The public humiliation makes them choose to die and spread the virus rather than seek help. Some can't afford to go to clinics that are outside their residential areas because they are not working. This would mean that everyone in their community will know what diseases they have. We cannot pretend that the stigma attached to HIV is no longer there. People still feel scared to disclose their status, so they will not let the nurses do that on their behalf.

This is one of the main reasons why HIV/AIDS is still a pandemic, and it is spreading the way it is. If the number of people who were aware of their status were being treated, this disease would have been suppressed, meaning it would not have been easily transmissible. Now, even though people are aware of their statuses. They are scared to go to clinics and get tested or to collect medication.

When all this happens, why are the people who continue to undermine their jobs not charged and made an example of? We need to restore the "dignity" of our people, not just because of their financial standing, but let us try to create a fair economy with equal rights. The apartheid regime came with the" divide and conquer" mentality by segregating people according to race, culture and financial status. The mandate of a democratic government is to rewrite history, ensuring that people are treated with fairness and equality.

The government have huge charts about Batho Pele principles, but the people who work there seem to forget them. To mention a few of those principles, they state that:

Government departments must establish clear service standards and communicate them effectively, so that people know what level of service to expect. Performance should be measured against these standards.

When services fall below promised standards, the government must offer an apology, explanation, and a solution. If mistakes are made, they should be corrected quickly.

The Batho Pele Principles prioritise the needs of citizens; they were designed to foster trust in government and enhance service delivery following the end of apartheid.

The public healthcare needs a whole makeover because it is currently in such a state, it is a shocker because most of the hospitals were built in the apartheid regime, yet the ones that we have are dilapidated and old. They require maintenance, and the lack of equipment is also a contributing factor to low staff morale. It is an absolute nightmare to work with little equipment, and with an influx of people looking at you straight in the eye.

Patients wait hours to be seen at clinics, and months or even years for specialist procedures.

Delays in test results and referrals often worsen health conditions, sometimes leading to deaths that could have been avoided.

The South African government is failing in public healthcare due to corruption, inadequate infrastructure, and significant disparities between the public and private sectors. While the Constitution promises health care as a right, in practice, millions of South Africans receive inadequate services.

The Freedom Charter envisioned that every person, regardless of race or income, would have equal access to healthcare. This links to the constitutional rights of dignity, equality, and human rights, as well as better living conditions, to promote health.

The Charter promised *"free medical care and hospitalisation for all"*, yet today millions still face barriers to quality, primary healthcare. Mothers and children continue to face high risks, especially in rural areas where maternity wards and ambulances are scarce.

The vision of the charter is faced with the realities of how government fails in public when it comes to healthcare; this is a betrayal of one of the liberation struggle's core promises.

The Freedom Charter imagined healthcare as a tool of equality. The persistent inequality and corruption show how far South Africa still is from realising this dream. The disparity between *promises made* and *promises delivered* makes healthcare a powerful lens through which we can measure the successes and failures of post-apartheid governance.

With the arrival of democracy in 1994, many South Africans believed that the Charter's promise was finally being fulfilled. Important progress was made, free primary health care was introduced, thousands of new clinics were built, and South Africa became home to the world's largest HIV/AIDS treatment programme. The 1996 Constitution went further, enshrining in law the right of everyone to access healthcare services.

Yet, despite these strides, the reality of public healthcare today stands in painful contrast to the vision of the Freedom Charter.

Failures of SASSA and other Social Grant Systems

The Social Grant in South Africa is A Safety Net with Holes

According to the 2024 National Treasury Budget review, South Africa's grant system is one of the country's largest anti-poverty instruments. Excluding the COVID-era Social Relief of Distress Grant (Covid-19 SRD grant), the National

Treasury projected that the core beneficiary base would rise from 18.8 million (2023/24) to 19.7 million over the medium term, primarily driven by population ageing and high unemployment.

Grants are also a major budget line, with social protection exceeding R300 billion in 2024/25, with old age and child support grants being the two largest items. Treasury's 2025 review still shows the social wage expanding but warns that "reform and efficiency savings" are needed to keep the system sustainable.

South Africa's social grant system, administered primarily through the South African Social Security Agency (SASSA), was created to protect the most vulnerable citizens to alleviate poverty. Grants such as the Child Support Grant, Old Age Pension, Disability Grant, and the more recent Social Relief of Distress (SRD) R350 grant have provided critical income to millions of households. Yet, despite its good intention, the SASSA system has repeatedly revealed deep fractures in administration, corruption and policy direction. Instead of acting as a stable lifeline, SASSA has often been an epicentre of corruption.

The important role played by Grants in South Africa

Grants are not a privilege in South Africa; they are a constitutional right. With unemployment staggering over 30% more than 18 million South Africans rely on grants to survive. For many rural and low-income families, grants make a significant difference because they provide the means to put food on the table. In this context, corruption by SASSA officials is not only a crime, but they are also standing between the life and death of every South African who benefits from it.

Administrative Failures and Scandals

SASSA has a long history of mismanagement:

In 2017, the Constitutional Court ruled that SASSA's contract with Cash Paymaster Services (CPS) was invalid, yet millions of grants were still paid through CPS. This exposed deep errors in tender processes and created conditions where private companies profited from poverty through unfair service fees and deductions from beneficiaries' accounts.

Delays and System Crashes: Beneficiaries often queue for hours, only to find that SASSA systems are offline. This seems to be one of the Government offices' norms, the system crash is a widespread phenomenon. The government always fail to invest in systems that can withstand thousands of people queuing for help. Elderly and disabled citizens are particularly affected because they are forced to travel long distances only to be turned away.

Verification Failures: Applicants are frequently rejected for grants due to "system errors" or faulty verification against Home Affairs databases, leading to wrongful rejections.

Covid-19 SRD Grant: A Symbol of Dysfunction

The R350 SRD grant was introduced during the COVID-19 pandemic for all unemployed South Africans; it is perhaps the most glaring example of government failure. While it provided hope for the unemployed, its rollout was tarnished by:

- Many deserving applicants were unfairly rejected due to minor technicalities, such as having received a small bank deposit, which the system incorrectly interpreted as "income."

- **Payment Delays**: Months-long backlogs left millions without support during lockdowns. This is another sad reality, to the extent that delays have become normalised when the government is involved.

- **Digital Divide**: The online application system excluded those without internet access, smartphones.

Intervention is poorly implemented; this escalates suffering rather than alleviating it, especially for those people who are now dependent on the grant.

Corruption and Exploitation

The SASSA system has also been a fertile ground for corruption:

- **Fake Beneficiaries**: Ghost beneficiaries and fraudulent claims milk billions from the fiscus, while legitimate claimants are rejected.

- **Corruption**: Reports of officials demanding bribes to fast-track applications or process claims.

All this failure translates to consistent human pain and suffering, making the poor remain poorer and the rich richer. You can always see SASSA cards of these ghost beneficiaries being confiscated, but why are there no strict rules to ensure that this never happens again? Imagine the millions of rands that are being looted on a monthly basis. Those who are caught are just the tip of the iceberg.

Political Accountability and Governance Failure

The failures of SASSA are not simply administrative; they are political. Repeated court interventions show how government departments ignore constitutional obligations until forced by litigation. Parliament's oversight is weak, with portfolio committees unwilling to take responsibility, instead shifting blame; this results in a lack of accountability. And they are often more reactive than proactive. Ministers in charge of Social Development frequently promise reform, yet fundamental issues remain unresolved.

Structural Problems in the Welfare System

SASSA's failures also reveal deeper issues in the broader South African welfare system:

How can a single agency be tasked with servicing millions without adequate resources?

Slow adoption of efficient digital systems, they should invest more in cybersecurity and fraud detection.

One of the biggest failures of the grants system is that it creates dependence on Grants Without Job Creation. While grants alleviate poverty, they do not address unemployment, leaving citizens permanently dependent on a flawed system.

- Increased poverty and hunger when grants are delayed or denied.

- Loss of trust in government institutions.

- Wasted taxpayer money on administrative inefficiency.

For SASSA to fulfil its constitutional mandate, radical reforms are required:

- Strengthening oversight and accountability at ministerial and parliamentary levels.

- Investing in vigorous digital infrastructure and anti-fraud systems.

- Ensuring transparent tender processes.

- Integrating SASSA systems with banks.

- Restructuring social protection to job creation and education, rather than permanent dependency.

SASSA embodies both the promise and the failure of post-apartheid governance. One cannot turn a blind eye and pretend that grants did not lift millions out of extreme poverty, but mismanagement and corruption have left many destitute. A state that cannot reliably protect its most vulnerable citizens proves its deepest crisis of legitimacy. Until the government treats SASSA as a priority institution worthy of professionalism, the poor will continue to suffer, and the dream of a truly just society will remain unfulfilled.

Many failures of our government are shielded by the term "UBUNTU"; we have normalised the term such that we misuse it. We must know where we draw the line; if all the companies were run with the spirit of ubuntu as we know it, they wouldn't be sustainable. We have done so many things in our country that are unconstitutional, in the name of Ubuntu, it is culturally unheard of to let a starving person go simply because they do not belong in your family, some of us were raised by who fed families and lived with children who were not theirs, this is why many members of parliament carried that same mentality, we must know when the spirit of ubuntu is overly exercised. Similar to the issue of social grants, these benefits are reserved for South Africans, including free education and free healthcare. Anyone who is not a South African citizen by birth or naturalisation is not supposed to enjoy these benefits, no matter how dire their situation is. Non-South Africans must pay for their education and their healthcare. Try visiting other countries, and you will see how you have to pay for each and every service, and the same people from these countries expect to be treated differently when it comes to our country. Why? Because as a country, we do not know where to draw the line.

I watched the news the other day, and there was a lady who leads a group of radical South Africans who are protecting our country from illegal immigrants who seem to have taken over. These are patriots who are trying to ensure that we protect what we still call ours, the discussion on the news was about the march and march officials who are blocking foreigners from accessing hospitals, the news anchor then says, but our constitution according to a document sent by the human rights commission states that everyone has a right to primary healthcare and this includes South Africans, refugees, Asylum seekers as well as foreigners, documented and undocumented migrants as well as stateless persons, this made me pause and do my own investigation to see which part of the institution mentions that, the lady then responded with calmness and facts, she quoted that our constitution talks about everyone, and it depends on how you interpret everyone, but it doesn't mention documented and undocumented, well I made my own research and found that section 27.1 of the constitution does mention that everyone has a right to primary health care, but nowhere does it mention documented and undocumented! This came as a shock to me to hear a news anchor who didn't bother to do any research before spewing unfounded information. This is a reflection of the ignorance of our people, quick to respond. Quick to write posts and have discussions about improperly researched topics.

The lady had done her thorough research, and she spoke with great eloquence because you can't address people if you yourself don't believe in what you are saying. These are the kinds of leaders our country needs, not people who will present speeches that don't make sense, and when you question them, they start mumbling words. We need to stand up for our country and ensure that the next generation finds this country still intact. It is sad to see it dwindling away right before our eyes.

The constitution should serve as a document that protects our people from being exploited. In fact, everyone in South Africa should have a copy of the constitution. There was a time in our country when printed copies of the Constitution were distributed to every household. You can visit any government institution and find copies available for public consumption. It is no longer the case; hence, people don't know the Constitution off by heart.

Our country should be led by people who are not apologetic when it comes to the truth. Why do we have leaders who change with the weather? Our country is a diverse community, and it should be led in a way that accommodates every skin colour. Not just a group of people.

One of the main issues that we face as a country is comrades calling each other comrades. We are not against it; maybe they are, but this nullifies accountability, it makes them protect each other even when they are wrong. They feel like they owe each other favours, hence we see our leaders committing crimes left, right and centre, but none of them goes to jail for the crimes they have committed; instead, like I mentioned earlier, they get redeployed. The reshuffling of the cabinet and redeployment are the reasons why we will constantly have incompetent leaders in the government. If a person has proven themselves to be incompetent leaders, then what difference does reshuffling them make?

The government has lost its way; it is no longer there to serve the country, but has become a money-making scheme and an employment entity. The government shouldn't be a place for people to become richer; it should be a place where people hold office to serve the people, but it has become a hub for looting funds. People who work for the government are not even allowed to open their own businesses, but if you peel one layer off all the businesses that are receiving huge tenders, you'd be surprised to know that most of them belong to the very officials who issue these tenders. Then you wonder, how can their income afford them the luxurious lifestyles that they lead? Nobody is willing to talk about that.

The Impact of COVID-19 on Health Inequities

COVID-19 (Coronavirus Disease 2019) is an infectious disease caused by the severe acute respiratory syndrome coronavirus 2 (SARS-CoV-2), which was first identified in Wuhan, China, in December 2019. It spread rapidly across the world, leading the World Health Organization (WHO) to declare it a global pandemic in March 2020.

When COVID-19 hit South Africa in March 2020, it exacerbated the numerous problems already present in our country, leaving the country unstable and worse off than it was before. The pandemic arrived in a country already defined by staggering health inequities shaped by decades of

Robert Mzimela

apartheid's racial exclusion, worsening poverty, and a democratic government that has promised transformation. Instead of confronting these inequalities head-on, the government's response to COVID-19 exposed the cracks in **the health system and widened the gap between the haves and the have-nots.**

The pandemic was never "the great equalizer," as most people claimed. In South Africa, it was the great divider. The wealthy quarantined in spacious homes with access to private healthcare, medical aids, and secure jobs that moved online, but it was not the same phenomenon for a simple father who had to provide food on the table through general work that couldn't be "taken home" or moved to an online platform. Millions in townships and informal settlements faced impossible choices: obey lockdown regulations or put food on the table.

The government's harsh restrictions did not account for overcrowding, lack of clean water, or reliance on informal work. Police brutality became the enforcement tool of choice in poor communities, echoing apartheid-era enforcement, where people who carried on with their lives were bullied, arrested, and life had to change rapidly in an instant, while in leafy suburbs, curfews were an inconvenience, not a death sentence. COVID-19 turned inequality from a background reality into a frontline battle. It was a nightmare, if you were not born during the apartheid regime, COVID-19 replayed those scenarios very well, the only difference was that the people who enforced these strict rules were no longer white on blacks, it was black on black war!

An Overburdened Health System

The pandemic exposed the shortcomings of the public health sector. The system struggled under the weight of COVID-19 cases. Shortages of oxygen, ventilators, and basic protective gear were nothing new; they just worsened. These were the results of years of corruption, cadre deployment, and funds mismanagement.

Frontline workers protested without PPE, clinics in the rural areas turned patients away, and hospitals needed resources. For the elite, private hospitals and medical aid schemes boasted survival. For the poor, state hospitals became a hub for the sick and the dying. The government's unpreparedness for a crisis was laid bare.

Vaccines and the Politics of Access

When vaccines arrived, South Africa gladly proved that political failure is as deadly as the virus itself. Procurement was slow, negotiations with pharmaceutical companies dragged on, and again, nothing new there. In the early phases, vaccination centres were concentrated in urban areas, leaving rural and township populations ignored.

The "people's government" once again privileged insiders while the majority waited in long lines, often being sent home due to shortages. Vaccine hesitancy was not merely ignorance; it was a rational response to decades of betrayal by a government that treats the poor with less urgency.

Social Relief or Social Control?

The government's much-publicized COVID-19 Social Relief of Distress Grant (SRD) was framed as a lifeline. But in practice, it became another symbol of dysfunction. Payments were delayed for months, and eligibility rules excluded millions of deserving people in distress.

In the midst of all those struggles, the country faced, politically connected businesses benefited millions through PPE contracts, proving once again that in South Africa, crisis is an opportunity for the well-connected and a pathway for corruption.

COVID-19 was not just a health crisis; it was a political crisis that exposed the inadequacies of our national disaster preparedness. The government's failures cannot be excused by the pandemic. Other middle-income countries managed faster vaccine rollouts and more equitable relief. South Africa's crisis was deepened by its own leaders' inability or unwillingness to prioritise the needs of ordinary citizens over personal interests. In the end, COVID-19 reflected the state's desertion of its constitutional promise of "health care for all."

COVID-19 revealed a brutal truth: South Africa has two health systems, one for the rich and one for the poor. The pandemic should have been the moment to correct these injustices, to prioritize public health, and to deliver dignity to the poor.

Instead, the government's response established inequality and demonstrated that political failure can be as deadly as any virus.

The pandemic may have passed, but the inequities it exposed remain. The government needs to move beyond the empty promises to action.

Chapter 6

Corruption: Erosion of

Trust in Democratic Institutions

The Impact of Corruption on Governance and Service Delivery

Democratic Governance is built on trust. Citizens surrender power to elected representatives in the belief that the state will protect their rights, deliver services, and manage resources in the public interest. However, in South Africa, corruption has eroded this trust. Instead of being a tool for equality, the state has become a means for political leaders and their networks to generate wealth. The result is an erosion of trust and a failure in service delivery, as well as growing disillusionment with the so-called democratic government.

The Roots of Betrayal

Corruption in South Africa did not start overnight. It dates back to the apartheid regime. The promise of liberation in 1994 was that democratic governance would end these injustices. Yet instead of dismantling the old tactics, new ones were built, often under the banner of "democracy."

Things like the Black Economic Empowerment (BEE), meant to correct racial inequalities, but since its inception, it has become a shield for politically connected elites to snatch state contracts. Transformation was hijacked by 'tenderpreneurs', while the majority remained stuck in poverty. The state became less about service delivery and more about who gets awarded what tender.

State Capture: The Turning Point

The Zuma era (2009–2018) often addressed the peak of institutionalized corruption. The phenomenon of state capture, exposed by whistleblowers, journalists, and later the Zondo Commission, revealed how private families, such as the Guptas, effectively directed government decisions, from cabinet appointments to billion-rand contracts.

This was not small corruption. It was systemic looting of public resources that crippled state-owned enterprises, drained the fiscus to the core, and destroyed professional governance. The message to ordinary citizens was clear: democracy serves only a select minority.

Municipalities collapse due to mismanagement and, of course, theft. Rubbish goes uncollected, water infrastructure decays, electricity supply falters, and roads disintegrate. Communities protest against the absence of basic services. The most amusing aspect of this is that most corrupt municipalities consistently produce clean audits. Why? I think you know the answer to that.

Every misallocated tender translates into fewer clinics and other services that would have benefited millions of South Africans who are still living in dire poverty. In healthcare, corruption manifested in PPE scandals during the COVID-19 pandemic, where billions earmarked for saving lives were stolen in broad daylight. To this day, nobody has taken accountability for what happened to those funds that were looted during the pandemic. In education, it meant undelivered textbooks in Limpopo. In housing, it meant RDP homes built with sand that collapse on families. Corruption is not without victims; it kills. I don't know how people who steal funds meant to develop the country sleep at night.

The Collapse of Trust

When leaders loot with freedom, citizens lose faith in democracy itself. Surveys indicate a declining voter turnout, particularly among young people, who are increasingly viewing elections as meaningless rituals. Can we blame them? The last elections showed how unsure people are when it comes to voting. The ANC lost its former glory, and we saw Umkhonto we Sizwe taking elections by storm, because people believed in the former President Zuma. Before you assume I have any political affiliation, please note that this book focuses on government as a whole, rather than just party politics. The once-dominant ANC suffered a significant blow in 2024, but opposition parties, too, are not immune to accusations of corruption. The result is the belief that all politicians are thieves and that government cannot be trusted.

This erosion of trust weakens democratic institutions. Law enforcement agencies, such as the Hawks and the NPA, were compromised. Even Chapter Nine institutions, designed to safeguard democracy, faced political interference.

The impact of corruption extends beyond financial loss to political decay. Democracy loses its moral authority when leaders betray the trust of the people. South Africa now faces a legitimacy crisis: can citizens continue to place faith in institutions that repeatedly fail them? How can the ANC return to its former glory?

Corruption erodes not only today's services but also tomorrow's possibilities. It undermines investment, drives away skills, and embeds inequality. The poor suffer the most, but ultimately, the entire society pays the price of a state that cannot govern effectively.

For South Africa, fighting corruption is not just about punishing a few individuals; it is about rebuilding trust in democracy itself. Without accountability, transparent governance, and leaders who prioritise public interests over personal gain, service delivery will remain broken, and democratic institutions will continue to wither.

The people of South Africa fought too hard for liberation to see democracy stolen by corruption. The question now is whether the political will exists to confront this betrayal, or whether the erosion of trust will continue until the people lose faith in democracy altogether.

Case Studies of High-Profile Corruption Scandals

The VBS Bank Collapse

The 2018 VBS Mutual Bank scandal shocked the entire nation. It was promoted as a "people's bank" for poor communities, but instead was looted by politicians. Over R2 billion was looted, leaving depositors, including pensioners and rural villagers, destitute. It served as another scheme for politicians to enrich themselves in the name of serving the people.

The collapse of VBS emphasized how corruption preys on the poor, stripping them not only of money but of dignity. This was a symbol that no institution was safe from political theft.

The PPE Scandal during COVID-19

At the peak of the pandemic, when South Africans were dying in congested hospitals, Personal Protective Equipment (PPE) tenders became yet another money-making scheme for the connected few. Billions meant for masks, gloves, and sanitizers were looted through inflated contracts, ghost suppliers, and politically linked companies.

Instead of saving lives, corruption turned COVID-19 into a business opportunity. Frontline workers protested without adequate equipment, and ordinary people were left with a stark reality: absolutely no institution is safe. Imagine robbing people of money that is meant to save their lives. How cold can one be?

Public Response and Calls for Accountability

In a democratic country, the people's voice is the ultimate check on power. When leaders fail, citizens are not silent. Public anger has overflowed onto the streets and across social media, demanding accountability from a government that too often hides behind slogans while dodging responsibility. South Africa's recent history reveals a population that is unwilling to accept betrayal, even as corruption, mismanagement, and inequality deepen.

Protests as the Politics of Last Resort

South Africa is left with no choice but to protest, as it appears that public outcry often falls on deaf ears. Communities rise up daily against collapsing service delivery, corruption in municipalities, and broken promises of housing, water, and electricity. These protests are rarely spontaneous; they are a cry for help and attention, they are a desperate measure. Citizens protest because formal democratic channels have failed to address their concerns.

From township barricades to student movements like #FeesMustFall, protests have become the candid instrument of demanding accountability. Yet instead of listening, the state often responds with police brutality and rubber bullets; this is the response that was learnt from the apartheid government. When people were tired of abuse, they resorted to the streets, and they were dispersed using rubber bullets and teargas. It is exhausting to see that the struggle of a black child still continues. The message to the poor is clear: democracy is celebrated at the ballot box but suppressed in the streets.

Civil Society and the Fight Against State Capture

While politicians looted, civil society organizations became watchdogs of democracy. Groups like Corruption Watch, OUTA (Organisation Undoing Tax Abuse), and the Helen Suzman Foundation dragged government officials to court, exposing scandals.

The Zondo Commission of Inquiry into State Capture only happened because journalists, whistleblowers, and activists refused to let corruption be swept under the carpet. Testimonies of shameless looting shocked the nation, but more importantly, they mobilized citizens to demand justice. For many, the Commission symbolized both the rot in the state and the resilience of democracy when citizens refuse to be silent.

Media and Whistleblowers: Guardians of Truth

South Africa's investigative journalists, like Daily Maverick and News24, have often been the first line of accountability. It was journalists who revealed the Guptas' influence, the VBS bank collapse, and the COVID-19 PPE scandals. Whistleblowers, often at great risk, have exposed internal corruption, despite the country having no protection plan for whistleblowers. We have witnessed many whistleblowers who died for exposing the truth; they died because we live in a country where criminals are protected and good citizens pay the price. Some, like Babita Deokaran, paid with their lives for daring to challenge theft in the health sector. South Africa should have done better to protect these patriots who risked their lives to ensure the resources of the state are protected, but they were exposed to the world of monsters that were ready to devour them for speaking out. Many whistleblowers have died for the truth, and what does our government do to ensure that their safety is guaranteed? Nothing.

For that reason, now it is hard for people when they are faced with crime in their workspaces, in fear of falling victim and losing their lives. Therefore, corruption will likely continue because people fear that if they speak out, they will become a victim.

The public's trust in the media has grown immensely because political institutions have failed. Where Parliament failed to hold the executives accountable, journalists and whistleblowers stepped into the gap.

Public Anger at the Ballot Box

Protests and court battles are not the only responses. At the 2024 general election, the African National Congress (ANC) lost its majority of voters for the first time since its 1994 election victory. Voters punished the ruling party for decades of corruption, unemployment, and failing services. The result was a Government of National Unity, a coalition that reflected deep public anger and rejection of one-party domination.

The ballot became a weapon of accountability. Citizens may be disappointed by politicians, but they used democracy's most powerful tool to show that betrayal has consequences.

Despite commissions of inquiry, court judgments, and political shifts, accountability remains obscure. Many implicated leaders still hold office, but very few are held accountable for their crimes in prison. This gap between exposure and punishment fuels contempt: South Africans have seen the truth, but they haven't seen justice being served. Our court systems have been captured by corrupt individuals.

Calls for accountability continue to echo across the country. Communities demand service delivery. Students demand education reform. Workers demand jobs. Whistleblowers demand protection. At the heart of all these struggles lies a single demand: that those who hold power must serve the people, not themselves.

Chapter 7

Social Justice: Inequality and Poverty

The Persistent Divide: Wealth and Income Inequality

Wealth and income inequality remain two of the most pressing challenges in the pursuit of social justice. While economic growth has lifted millions out of poverty globally, the distribution of resources has become increasingly concentrated in the hands of a small minority. This "persistent divide" between the wealthy and the poor threatens social cohesion, limits opportunities, and reinforces disadvantage to the already disadvantaged.

Income inequality refers to disparities in wages, salaries, and other forms of earnings, while wealth inequality reflects differences in accumulated assets, such as property, savings, and investments. Wealth is often more unequally distributed than income because it builds over generations and benefits from mechanisms such as inheritance and access to credit. Thus, wealth inequality entrenches privilege, while income inequality often reflects present-day labour market conditions.

Causes of the Divide

Several factors drive the persistent divide:

1. High-skilled workers and business owners benefit disproportionately from technological advancements, while low-skilled workers face job insecurity and stagnant wages.

2. Access to good, quality education is unequally distributed, perpetuating gaps in earning potential.

3. Race, gender, and class-based barriers reduce opportunities for marginalized groups, resulting in structural inequalities. We discussed this earlier in the book.

Consequences of Inequality

Persistent inequality has both social and economic consequences:

- When large sections of society feel excluded, it can lead to protests and political instability.

- Wealth concentration often translates into disproportionate political influence for elites, undermining fairness in governance.

- For those at the bottom, inequality reduces access to education, healthcare, and economic mobility, keeping them locked in cycles of poverty. The rich get richer, and the poor get poorer.

- Slower economic growth: South Africa had the potential to be a first-world country, but the mismanagement and corruption will keep us where we are, and it is so concerning that we have to be a safe haven for all the people who have lost hope in their countries to come here to look for greener pastures. Why do we continue to allow this? Do we have an agreement with these countries that we will continue serving their people at our own people's expense, what do we owe them, because they don't definitely don't owe us the same favours because when we go to these countries, they don't treat us like queens and kings, they want us to account why we are there and how long are we planning to be there for. Yet here, they call us xenophobic; this is the term that they use when they want to silence South Africans for asking important questions.

Addressing the Divide

Bridging the wealth and income divide requires smart strategies:

- Progressive taxation and wealth redistribution to ensure that the wealthy contribute fairly to social development.

- Universal access to quality education and healthcare to equalize opportunities, with the amount of money being looted, this should be possible.

- Inclusive labour market policies, such as living wages, skills training, and protection for vulnerable workers, need to address the exploitation of workers due to their race and gender. This continues to marginalise people, and there are those who are constantly at the bottom of the food chain. This needs to be addressed.

- Promoting equity in ownership and entrepreneurship so that wealth creation opportunities are accessible to wider divisions of the population. Entrepreneurship must be promoted because it will help with the rate of high unemployment.

Wealth and income inequality are not just economic issues but moral and social justice concerns.

A society that tolerates extreme inequalities risks undermining fairness, human dignity, and stability. Addressing the persistent divide requires both structural reforms and a commitment to policies that prioritize equity, ensuring that prosperity is shared across all groups.

The Role of Social Grants and Support Systems

Social grants and support systems are crucial tools in addressing poverty and mitigating the effects of inequality. They serve as redistributive mechanisms through which the state and other institutions transfer resources to the most vulnerable, ensuring a minimum standard of living and fostering social stability.

Purpose and Importance

Social grants are designed to:

- Alleviate poverty by providing income support to individuals and households who are unable to meet basic needs.

- Promote social justice by reducing the structural disadvantages faced by marginalized groups such as children, the elderly, and people with disabilities.

- Promote economic activity as grant recipients spend directly in local communities, thereby boosting demand for goods and services.

Support systems must include access to proper healthcare, education subsidies, housing assistance, and food programmes, all of which help break cycles of poverty and inequality.

Global and South African Context

Globally, countries adopted various forms of social protection, from unemployment insurance in developed economies. For example, Brazil's Bolsa Família programme ties grants to school attendance and healthcare visits, aiming to reduce intergenerational poverty.

In South Africa, social grants form a crucial foundation for poverty alleviation, particularly given the country's extremely high levels of inequality. Administered by the South African Social Security Agency (SASSA), these include:

- Old Age Pension for elderly citizens.

- Child Support Grant for Primary Caregivers of Children.

- Disability Grant for individuals unable to work due to illness or impairment.

- Foster Child and Care Dependency Grants for vulnerable children.

As of 2025, over 18 million South Africans rely on social grants, making them one of the largest redistributive mechanisms in the country. The temporary COVID-19 Social Relief of Distress Grant (SRD) highlighted their role in cushioning households against economic shocks and unemployment.

Challenges and Limitations

Despite their importance, grants and support systems face several challenges:

1. **Sustainability** – Rising fiscal pressure questions whether governments can expand or maintain such programmes. There have been discussions about the discontinuation of social grants. This would have caused a serious uproar because that money is the lifeline between life and death. We all know that even graduates are sitting at home with no jobs because securing a job in South Africa has become harder over the years.

2. **Dependency concerns** – Critics argue grants may discourage employment, although evidence often shows they supplement rather than replace incomes.

3. **Exclusion errors** – Not all eligible individuals successfully access grants due to administrative factors.

Moving forward to strengthen the role of grants and support systems, governments and societies should:

- Foster skills development and employment opportunities, the government must ensure that employment opportunities are available to avoid recipients' dependency on grants.

- Expand complementary services such as free education, subsidised healthcare, and affordable housing as an aim to fight poverty.

- Adopt inclusive economic policies that reduce reliance on grants by creating sustainable livelihoods.

Social grants and support systems are vital instruments of social justice. They provide immediate relief from poverty and reduce inequality, particularly in contexts such as South Africa, where economic disparities are stark. However, for lasting impact, they must be combined with long-term structural reforms that expand opportunity and address the root causes of economic exclusion.

Movements for Social Justice and Their Impact

In South Africa, social justice movements are slowly dismantling structural inequality and challenging poverty:

- **The Anti-Apartheid Struggle** – The Freedom Charter (1955) articulated a vision of equality, land redistribution, and access to education and healthcare, values that are still echoed in today's Constitution.

- **Trade Unions** – Movements such as the Congress of South African Trade Unions (COSATU) have advocated for workers' rights, fair wages, and protections, influencing labour legislation in the democratic era.

- **#FeesMustFall (2015–2017)** – A student-led movement demanding affordable and accessible higher education. It pressured the government to stop tuition hikes and expand financial aid through NSFAS, reshaping debates on educational equity.

- **Gender and LGBTQ+ Rights Movements** – Campaigns for gender equality and LGBTQ+ rights have expanded awareness, challenged patriarchal norms, and pushed for stronger protections against gender-based violence and discrimination. The gender-based violence has escalated in this country, and it continues to do so.

- The justice system should apply more stringent penalties for GBV. It starts with a slap in the face, then it escalates. South Africa mustn't just let it reach murder proportions; it must be nipped in the bud.

Impact of Social Justice Movements

The impact of these movements can be measured in several ways:

1. **Policy Change** – Many movements have directly led to new laws, reforms, and institutional changes, improving access to rights and services.

2. **Awareness and Public Debate** – By mobilizing the public, movements bring hidden injustices into mainstream discourse.

3. **Empowerment of Marginalized Groups** – Social movements provide a platform for the voices of those excluded from traditional political processes.

Challenges Faced by Movements

Despite their successes, social justice movements often face resistance:

- Such as police brutality, restrictive laws, or censorship.

- Structural barriers, including entrenched economic interests and global inequalities, are difficult to dismantle.

Movements for social justice are powerful drivers of change. They highlight the lived realities of inequality, unite communities under shared goals, and challenge deep-rooted systems of power. In South Africa and around the globe, their impact demonstrates that progress toward equality and poverty reduction is not solely a product of policy, but also of persistent civic engagement, activism, and solidarity.

Chapter 8

Freedom of Speech and Press:

A Democratic Dilemma

The Importance of Free Expression in a Democracy

Freedom of speech and freedom of the press are often described as the essence of democracy. They provide citizens with the ability to question authority, criticize government actions, and advocate for social and political change without fear of censorship. A democracy thrives on the active participation of its people, and such participation is only possible when citizens have access to diverse information and are free to express differing views.

Safeguarding Accountability

One of the most significant functions of free expression is to hold leaders accountable. When individuals, journalists, are free to investigate and publish information, corruption, abuse of power, and inefficiency are more likely to be exposed. This transparency strengthens trust in democratic institutions.

Promoting an Informed Citizenry

Democracy relies on informed citizens making rational decisions about policies, leaders, and national priorities. Free expression ensures that ideas, popular or controversial, are openly debated, allowing people to consider multiple perspectives before forming their conclusions. The issue we face in South Africa is that manifestos are often delivered in English, which creates a barrier for those who do not understand the language. Because we go around delivering speeches in black communities, it is only fair that when the gathering has a certain command of the audience, a certain language is used to bridge misunderstandings. The documents may then be made available for those who didn't understand at that particular time.

Protecting Minority Voices

A robust democracy is not defined solely by majority rule, but also by its protection of minority rights.

Free expression allows marginalized groups to advocate for equality and reform. Throughout history, movements for civil rights, gender equality, and social justice have relied on the ability to speak freely and challenge mainstream or oppressive norms.

Balancing Rights and Responsibilities

Although essential, freedom of expression is not absolute. Democracies often face the dilemma of balancing free speech with the need to prevent hate speech, incitement to violence, or the spread of harmful misinformation. The challenge lies in drawing boundaries that protect public order and dignity while avoiding unjust censorship.

In essence, free expression is both a right and a responsibility. It sustains the democratic process by ensuring accountability, promoting informed decision-making, and protecting diversity of thought. Censorship paves the way for authoritarianism.

Challenges Faced by Journalists and Activists

While freedom of speech and the press are essential to democracy, those who exercise these rights often encounter significant challenges. Journalists and activists, in particular, play a critical role in uncovering truth and amplifying marginalized voices, but they frequently face obstacles that limit their effectiveness and sometimes threaten their safety.

In many democracies, governments attempt to control narratives by imposing restrictions on media outlets and activists. This can take the form of direct censorship, denial of broadcasting licenses, or elusive pressures such as withholding advertising revenue. Political leaders may also stigmatize journalists as "enemies of the people" to undermine their credibility, which corrodes public trust in the press.

Journalists and activists often risk intimidation, online harassment, and even physical attacks for their work. In extreme cases, investigative reporters or whistle-blowers have been imprisoned or killed for exposing corruption, human rights abuses, or powerful interests. Such threats create fear that deters others from speaking out.

Independent journalism is under financial strain, as advertising revenue shifts to digital platforms. Many newsrooms lack resources to fund in-depth investigative reporting, leaving space for misinformation and propaganda to dominate.

Governments sometimes use restrictive laws. such as those against defamation, or "fake news", to suppress opposition. Surveillance technologies also pose a significant threat, allowing authorities to monitor communications, track movements, and target journalists with arrests. These practices discourage transparency and silence critical voices. This has always been the case, even during the apartheid government, where reporters were harassed and their equipment taken away.

The rise of social media has created both opportunities and dangers. While activists and journalists can reach wider audiences, they must also contend with disinformation campaigns and "fake news" that confuse the public and erode their credibility. In some contexts, state-sponsored propaganda further undermines trust in independent voices. Social media has significantly impacted news reporting, as the prevalence of fake news requires a considerable amount of effort to ensure that the truth prevails. People spread fake news to distract from the news being reported, and those who don't research before posting a trend allow the fake news to spread like wildfire.

In certain societies, cultural taboos or traditional norms can limit the issues journalists and activists are able to address, such as gender rights, sexuality, or religious critique. Challenging these norms can lead to social exclusion, stigmatization, or community backlash.

The work of news reporters, journalists, and activists is essential for sustaining democracy, but it is often carried out under conditions of risk, uncertainty, and opposition. Overcoming these challenges requires strong legal protections, public support for independent media, and international solidarity to defend freedom of expression. Without these, the democratic promise of free speech and press remains incomplete.

The Role of Media in Shaping Public Discourse

The media serves as the bridge between citizens and the state, influencing how people understand political, economic, and social issues. In a democracy, the media serve not only as a channel for information but also as a powerful tool that shapes public opinion, debate, and ultimately, decision-making. Its role extends beyond reporting facts; it scaffolds narratives, highlights certain perspectives, and sets the agenda for public discussion.

The media plays a crucial role in determining which issues receive public attention. Through choices about headlines, airtime, and page space, media outlets prioritize certain topics while downplaying others. This "agenda-setting" function directs the public's focus and can influence policy debates. Even though the media plays a pivotal role in reporting accurate news, it can also be biased; they decide which news receives attention and which is ignored. This is often a cause for concern among the public because some news stories receive more attention than others, and are often used as a means to focus on one aspect while downplaying others.

By investigating and exposing misconduct, corruption, and abuse of power, the media acts as a watchdog that holds leaders accountable. High-profile investigative journalism has historically led to transformations, resignations, and stronger public oversight.

An inclusive media environment ensures that not only elites but also marginalized communities can share their experiences and perspectives. By amplifying different voices, the media promotes pluralism and strengthens the legitimacy of democratic debate. This role is especially important in multicultural societies where diverse groups seek representation.

Beyond politics, the media plays a significant role in shaping cultural values and national identity. The portrayal of issues such as gender equality, race relations, or environmental sustainability can influence how societies view themselves and what they aspire to become. Media thus plays both an informative and normative role in shaping collective perception and consciousness.

The rise of social media has democratised communication, allowing individuals to bypass traditional media gatekeepers. While this creates opportunities for wider participation, it also fragments public discourse, leading to the spread of misinformation, and this further complicates the media's ability to inform citizens responsibly.

The media's influence on public discourse is powerful and complex. It has the capacity to strengthen democracy by promoting accountability. At the same time, it carries the risk of bias and manipulation if not balanced by ethical standards and critical media literacy among citizens. Ultimately, a healthy democracy depends not only on free media but also on an engaged public capable of discerning truth from distortion. We cannot cancel social media completely because it has served as a platform to discuss matters of utmost importance without being censored and without fear of being cancelled. Although some regulation is required, because sometimes things do get out of hand. But so far, social media has brought to the foreground things that traditional media could not. Like the exposure of one of the Miss South Africa contestants who was of Nigerian descent, people started asking questions, only to find that the parents allegedly forged papers. There are many cases that we would not have been aware of had it not been for social media doing the Lord's work.

Grassroots Movements and Their Influence in South Africa

Introduction

Grassroots movements in South Africa have historically played a decisive role in shaping social, political, and economic change. Rooted in local communities and often led by ordinary citizens, these movements mobilize collective action to challenge inequality, injustice, and exclusion. They are vital to civil society because they ensure that marginalized voices are represented in national debates and that government institutions remain accountable to the people.

Historical Role of Grassroots Movements

During apartheid, grassroots organizations such as the United Democratic Front (UDF), trade unions, and local civic associations were central in resisting state oppression. They mobilized ordinary people through protests, strikes, and boycotts, laying the groundwork for the democratic transition. This history highlights the profound tradition of activism in South Africa and its enduring impact on civil society.

Post-1994 Context

In democratic South Africa, grassroots activism remains a vital force. While formal democracy has given citizens voting rights and representation, many communities still face poverty, unemployment, poor service delivery, and inequality.

Grassroots groups step into this gap by advocating for social justice and demanding better governance. Examples include:

- **Treatment Action Campaign (TAC)**: successfully pressured the government to roll out HIV/AIDS treatment.

- **Abahlali baseMjondolo (Shack Dwellers' Movement):** campaigns for housing rights and against forced evictions.

- **Equal Education**: focuses on access to quality schooling, especially in under-resourced areas.

Influence on Policy and Society

Grassroots movements influence South Africa in several ways:

- Movements like TAC changed national health policy through court action and mass mobilization. Activist groups hold the government accountable for corruption, poor service delivery, and rights violations.

- By organizing at the local level, communities gain skills in leadership, negotiation, and advocacy, strengthening participatory democracy.

- Shaping Public Discourse: Movements frame key debates around land reform, gender equality, education, and climate justice.

Challenges Faced by Grassroots Movements

Despite their influence, grassroots activism faces serious challenges:

- Limited resources and funding.

- State repression, intimidation.

- Internal divisions and the difficulty of sustaining momentum.

Grassroots movements remain a vital part of South Africa's democracy, ensuring that development is people-centred and that the struggle for justice continues beyond the ballot box. They represent the conscience of civil society by challenging inequality, augmenting marginalized voices, and keeping the spirit of collective resistance that was inherited from the anti-apartheid struggle alive.

The Importance of Civic Engagement in Democracy

"Civic engagement ensures that all groups – including marginalized communities – have a voice in democratic processes. Without it, policies may favour only dominant groups. Engagement through grassroots organizations, social movements, and advocacy campaigns gives vulnerable citizens a platform to influence decision-making. For instance, the activism of student groups during the #FeesMustFall movement forced national attention on higher education inequality" (Luescher, Loader & Mugume, 2017).

Civic engagement is not optional in a democracy; it is essential. It strengthens accountability, ensures representation, builds trust, and empowers citizens to shape their own future. In South Africa, where inequality and social injustice remain pressing challenges, meaningful civic participation ensures that democracy delivers not just in form, but in substance, for all its people.

Case studies of successful activism

Introduction

South Africa's history of resistance and mobilization has produced powerful examples of activism that brought about meaningful social and political change. These case studies show how ordinary citizens, grassroots movements, and civil society organizations have successfully challenged inequality, influenced government policies, and defended human rights.

1. The Treatment Action Campaign (TAC)

One of the most successful activist movements in post-apartheid South Africa is the Treatment Action Campaign (TAC). Founded in 1998, TAC mobilized communities to demand access to life-saving HIV/AIDS treatment. Through legal challenges, mass protests, and international advocacy, the movement pressured the government to roll out antiretroviral (ARV) medication, despite initial resistance. In 2002, the Constitutional Court ordered the government to provide drugs for preventing mother-to-child transmission, a landmark victory that saved countless lives (Heywood, 2009).

TAC demonstrated how activism can directly change public health policy and strengthen constitutional rights.

2. Abahlali baseMjondolo (Shack Dwellers' Movement)

"Established in 2005, Abahlali baseMjondolo represents shack dwellers in Durban and other urban areas. The movement campaigns against forced evictions, poor housing conditions, and land allocation inequality. Despite facing harassment and state resistance, the group has won multiple court cases affirming the rights of poor communities to housing and dignity. By using grassroots mobilization, media advocacy, and legal strategies, Abahlali baseMjondolo has highlighted the ongoing housing crisis and the need for inclusive urban development" (Pithouse, 2013).

3. #FeesMustFall Student Movement

"The #FeesMustFall movement, which started in 2015, became one of the most significant youth-led activist campaigns in democratic South Africa. Students across the country protested against rising tuition fees, inadequate financial aid, and systemic inequality in higher education. The protests garnered national and international attention, prompting the government to freeze tuition fee increases in 2016 and expand funding through the National Student Financial Aid Scheme (NSFAS). Although challenges remain, the movement showed the power of coordinated, youth-driven activism in shaping education policy" (Langa, 2017).

4. March and March Movement

On 4 March 2025, a campaign was launched to advocate for South Africa's resources, which continue to be looted by illegal, undocumented immigrants. This march has become a vital pillar in the fight for justice, serving as a beacon of hope. Movements like these give us confidence that the future of our children is still in good hands, because there are people willing to take off their heels, put on takkies, and fight for what is rightfully ours.

Those behind the campaign have faced attempts to silence them. The leader of the movement was forcefully removed from her position as a popular radio DJ, but her relentlessness and patriotism did not deter her. South Africa must protect such individuals at all costs, because those who stand at the forefront of justice inevitably become enemies of criminals.

Meanwhile, our president remains safe under the protection of his blue-light entourage, while ordinary people on the ground are exposed to crime daily. It was shocking to hear him speak about the dilapidation of Johannesburg's CBD as if it were news to him. His focus seems fixed on international relations, but one must ask: how will that help a country rotting from within?

If you casually walk through suburbs that were once known for their affluence, where only the affluent resided, you would be shocked at their current condition. Parts of Durban that once stood as the pinnacle of the city are now littered with rubbish and filled with dilapidated buildings on the verge of collapse. Yet in this same country, citizens are branded xenophobic for pointing out how foreigners have hijacked our buildings.

Will this ever end? Who will save us if we do not stop everything and begin holding every single member of parliament accountable for the collapse of our country?

Chapter 9

Reimagining the Future:

Pathways to Realizing the Freedom Charter

Lessons Learned from Past Failures

The *Freedom Charter* of 1955 envisioned a South Africa based on equality, dignity, and justice. It promised that *"The People Shall Govern!"*, that there would be equal access to education, housing, healthcare, and that the country's wealth would benefit all. While we gained the illusion of freedom in 1994, our government has struggled to fully translate the Charter's vision into reality. Widespread poverty, inequality, corruption, and weak service delivery have led to growing cynicism among many South Africans.

South Africa remains one of the most unequal societies in the world. The Charter called for *"The People Shall Share in the*

Country's Wealth", but wealth distribution is still tilted in favour of a small elite. Millions remain unemployed, particularly the youth. Our youth must always be at the top of the list when we think of transformation; they are the future governors of the country, and if we don't take care of them, we shall have no country. We need to utilise their sharp minds and radical acts. Our freedom fighters were a group of young people who had great ideas and a sense of urgency. They stood up for the liberation of our people, but we have many who are still sitting in clubs and taverns. Young people today are discouraged and do not look forward to what the future has in store for them because they are struggling to find employment and feed their families. When they eventually secure jobs, they often lack training on how to manage their finances, and as a result, they make poor financial decisions.

The Freedom Charter also declared that *"The Doors of Learning and Culture Shall Be Opened"*. Yet, the public education system continues to struggle with overcrowded classrooms, underqualified teachers, and poor infrastructure. Rural and township schools often lack basic resources such as libraries, laboratories, and sanitation facilities. This hasn't changed even after 31 years of freedom.

One of the most significant failures of the democratic state has been endemic corruption. From state capture under the Zuma administration to ongoing scandals in municipalities and state-owned enterprises, corruption has drained resources meant for service delivery. This directly undermines the Charter's promise that *"All shall enjoy equal human rights"* because corruption diverts funds from basic services, such as water, electricity, and housing.

The Freedom Charter proclaimed that *"The Land Shall Be Shared Among Those Who Work It"* and that *"There Shall Be Houses, Security and Comfort"*. However, land reform has been slow and uneven, with most arable land still in the hands of a minority. Failed housing projects, mismanagement, and evictions contradict the Charter's promise of security and dignity. People are still living in great poverty. This shows that South Africa is taking its own sweet time to bring transformation. These failures undermine both economic growth and the basic rights promised in the Charter.

The South African government has made significant strides since 1994; however, the failures in addressing inequality, education, healthcare, housing, land reform, and corruption reveal a substantial gap between the *Freedom Charter's* vision and the present reality. These shortcomings suggest the need for reimagined routes. These failures must serve as lessons. They must teach the importance of accountability, inclusion, and civic engagement in society. Reimagining the future means re-committing to the Charter's ideals, not just in rhetoric but in practice, ensuring that freedom, dignity, and equality are realized for all South Africans.

Chapter 10

The role of politics in our society

The role that politics plays in our lives is as significant as that of religion. It is appalling that we live in a political world, yet our people know very little about what is happening in the world of politics.

This is not to say that this book focused only on politics, but we can't discuss the economy without mentioning politics, because we live in a political country. I think this topic has been discussed many times. I added my two cents, and hopefully, readers will be able to appreciate the perspective of an old, grey man who has nothing but hope that what's left can still be salvaged to serve the newer, growing, and upcoming generation.

Too often, political conversations in taxis, buses, or waiting rooms are heated but shallow. Opinions are exchanged without knowledge, and misinformation spreads quickly, especially on social media. One phrase taken out of context can fuel endless debate with no factual basis. This is why political education matters. If citizens fail to understand their own history and institutions, they leave themselves vulnerable to manipulation.

It happens to me all the time, and every time it does, I wonder whether it is due to ignorance or whether we've become accustomed to forming opinions about things we don't understand.

I wish, dear reader, you could take time to educate yourself on your topic of interest, and scrutinize information, dissect it and make it make sense to you before sharing it with others, and not involve yourself in discussions where you have little or no understanding at all.

What do we teach our children if we don't take the time to immerse ourselves in everything that takes place around, things that really matter to us?

In the world of social media, things are often taken out of context, and a single line can spark a discussion without a comprehensive body of knowledge. It is an absolute nightmare to hear people discussing something so important, yet spreading out-of-context and untrue information, which spreads like wildfire.

As I said, we need to pause and share truthful information, because it is so easy to spread information these days, with just a click of a button, a thousand people can see and consume it.

I know we live in a fast-paced world; digging into information sounds so outdated. Reading books and researching are things of the past. People want a few lines written and then conclude from there.

As the younger generation says, I will say this with my chest out and my chin up: politics play a huge role in our social welfare, and we all ought to know it as much as we know about the Sermon on the Mount.

Where do I even begin to talk about the current state of our country? It is our responsibility to ensure that South Africa doesn't become worse than it is today; we don't want to be strangers in our own homes.

We must discuss from a place of acquired knowledge and not venture into history we do not fully understand, for in doing so, we risk distorting it.

We must be careful not to erase or distort the sacrifices of those who came before us. Leaders such as Prince Mangosuthu Buthelezi and others in the liberation struggle did not endure hardship for nothing. Many sacrificed their freedom, time with their families, and even their lives so that South Africans today could inherit rights denied under apartheid

Black people formed a homeland government, one of which was the Inkatha ka Zulu, which took matters into their own hands. This was called the legislative assembly. Prince Mangosuthu Buthelezi didn't want to call it the legislature; it was *umkhandlu oshaya umthetho*.

The Boers didn't know how to ban a working government. In 1977, we thought they would abolish Inkatha, but they managed to continue fighting for the emancipation of our black people.

My interest was to focus on the cause of the government's failure, specifically the destruction of infrastructure, and the factors that led to riots, such as the Soweto uprising, where people were burning buildings. I never believed in the riots that led to property destruction because we will need these structures. The policy of destroying things is failing us, and as a result, it continues to happen today.

During the march, people destroyed buildings and infrastructure; that policy of protesting as a constitutional right is still affecting us, that policy of destroying things. The country is not governable; we experience numerous riots almost every day, and the shutdowns significantly impact the country's economy.

We don't want the same thing that happened in France during the French Revolution, which reshaped not only France but also the global political landscape. Its legacy is complex: it brought liberty, equality, and democratic ideals, yet it also highlighted the dangers of radicalism and unchecked violence. Ultimately, it remains a landmark moment in humanity's struggle for freedom and justice. The French

Revolution. The chaos, the strategy. Inside the country, people were doing nothing, so they started encouraging the youth to revolt.

Communism, we were all told that communism is the right thing, but is it a solution for a country like South Africa?

Communism: An Ideology of Equality?

Introduction

Communism is a political and economic ideology that seeks to establish a society where all property is collectively owned and wealth is distributed according to need. It emerged in the 19th century as a critique of capitalism and industrial society, developed most prominently by Karl Marx and Friedrich Engels in *The Communist Manifesto* (1848).

Core Principles of Communism

History is understood as a struggle between classes: the bourgeoisie (owners of production) and the proletariat (working class).

1. **Abolition of Private Property** – The means of production (land, factories, resources) are owned collectively by the people. Common Ownership – Economic resources are managed collectively to eliminate exploitation.

2. **Equality** – All individuals contribute according to their ability and receive according to their needs.

Historical Development

- **Karl Marx and Friedrich Engels** outlined communist theory as a response to the inequalities of capitalism.

- **Russian Revolution** (1917) – The Bolsheviks, led by Vladimir Lenin, established the first communist state (later the Soviet Union).

- **20th Century Spread** – Communism became influential in Eastern Europe, China (Mao Zedong), Cuba (Fidel Castro), and parts of Africa and Asia.

- **Cold War Era** (1947–1991) – The ideological struggle between capitalist democracies (led by the USA) and communist states (led by the USSR) dominated global politics.

Advantages (in theory)

- Promotes equality and social justice.

- Eliminates exploitation of workers.

- Provides universal access to basic needs (education, healthcare, housing).

- Encourages collective responsibility.

Criticisms and Failures

- Communist states often became oppressive, limiting freedoms.

- Centralized planning frequently led to shortages, waste, and stagnation.

- Opposition was often met with censorship, imprisonment, or violence.

- Collapse of the Soviet Union (1991) – Exposed the weaknesses of communist economies in competing with capitalist systems.

While traditional communism has declined, some countries (e.g., China, Cuba, Vietnam) still incorporate communist principles within hybrid systems. The ideology continues to influence debates on inequality, workers' rights, and capitalism.

Communism remains one of the most influential and controversial ideologies of modern history. It promised equality and liberation from exploitation, yet its implementation often resulted in authoritarianism and economic decline.

Is Communism Possible in South Africa?

1. Historical Context

South Africa has a long history of socialist and communist influence. The South African Communist Party (SACP), founded in 1921, played a key role in the struggle against apartheid. It worked in alliance with the African National Congress (ANC) and the trade union movement (COSATU) under the "Tripartite Alliance." The *Freedom Charter* of 1955 even carried socialist undertones, declaring that *"The people shall share in the country's wealth."*

However, after 1994, South Africa adopted a mixed economy that incorporated elements of capitalism (private property, foreign investment) and social welfare (grants, free basic services, affirmative action). This indicates that, although socialist ideas exist, the country has never fully adopted communism.

2. Theoretical Possibility

For communism to work in South Africa, several radical shifts would be required:

- Land reform would have to move beyond redistribution into communal/state ownership.

- Mines, banks, and energy companies would need to be nationalized.

- The elite and corporate structures would be dismantled, and resources would be shared more equally. (I doubt this would suffice.)

- Citizens would need to accept communal ownership over private accumulation of wealth.

In theory, South Africa has the natural resources (minerals, fertile land, human capital) that could support a socialist or communist model.

3. Practical Challenges

- Radical communism could lead to sanctions and isolation (as seen in Zimbabwe).

- State capture and corruption suggest that nationalization without accountability might enrich elites rather than ordinary citizens. As the case of Black economic empowerment (BEE).

- South Africa's inequality, racial tensions, and class divisions could make collective ownership difficult to implement fairly.

- Historical Precedents, as well as Experiences in SADC countries like Zimbabwe and Zambia, show that poorly implemented state control can harm economies.

4. Current Reality

Instead of full communism, South Africa follows a hybrid model:

- Social welfare programmes (grants, free healthcare for the poor).

- Affirmative action and BEE policies to redistribute opportunities.

- State ownership of strategic enterprises (Eskom, Transnet, SAA).

- Co-existence with private enterprise and foreign investment.

This is closer to social democracy or state capitalism than communism.

While communism is theoretically possible, it is highly unlikely in practice due to corruption and the risks of repeating the mistakes of countries like Zimbabwe and Zambia. A more realistic path is to strengthen social democracy by balancing private enterprise with redistribution, accountability, and robust social protections.

Chapter 11

From Royal Roots to Political Triumph:

The Untold Journey of Ulundi's First Mayor

Early Life and Royal Heritage

Mr. Muntuwekosi Robert Mzimela was born in 1945 in Emacekane, the third child of Phambumbayo Mzimela (son of the late iNkosi Ntshidi Mzimela) and MaNtanzi Mzimela. His lineage traces back to the Zulu royal family through significant historical connections: the late King Dinuzulu kaCetshwayo was the son of Nomvimbi Mzimela, establishing the enduring relationship between the Mzimela family and Zulu royalty.

The bond between the Mzimela and Buthelezi families runs deep in history. The late Inkosi Mathole Buthelezi, father of the late Prince Mangosuthu Buthelezi, maintained a close friendship with the late King Ntshidi Mzimela. This relationship would later prove significant in Mr Mzimela's professional career.

During his formative years, Mr Mzimela was nurtured at Thembalimbe by his aunt Mehlathathani, who was married into the Shembe family. This early exposure to different cultural and spiritual traditions would shape his understanding of community service and cultural preservation.

Educational Journey

Mr Mzimela's educational path took him through several institutions that laid the foundation for his future leadership roles. He attended eMbabe Primary School and Ongoye Primary School before completing his secondary education at Obambiswano Secondary High School in Eshowe, where he achieved first-class honours in 1969.

His pursuit of higher education marked a historic moment for his family. From 1971 to 1973, he attended the University of Zululand, where he earned a Bachelor of Arts degree— becoming the first family member to achieve university-level education and establishing a precedent for future generations. His academic excellence continued as he completed an honours degree in Psychology during 1974-1975.

The financial challenges of his first year were significant, but the introduction of bursaries in 1972 provided the support necessary to complete his studies. This experience with educational funding challenges would later influence his understanding of the barriers that aspiring students in his community face.

Early Career: Department of Community Affairs

On March 3, 1975, Mr Mzimela began his government career as a Grade 1 clerk with the Department of Community Affairs in Pietermaritzburg. His honours degree qualified him for a higher starting salary, reflecting the value placed on educational achievement within the emerging governmental structure.

The Department of Community Affairs, with its team of ten employees, held comprehensive responsibility for health and welfare services, including clinic operations and elderly care. Mr Mzimela's duties involved coordinating with pharmaceutical companies like Pfizer to procure medications and ensure their delivery to clinics throughout the region, which were typically managed by nursing staff.

One particularly memorable assignment involved delivering medications to the Ezakheni Clinic. The journey proved challenging when he encountered fuel shortages, requiring a magistrate's letter to obtain petrol. Poor signage beyond Estcourt led to him becoming lost, and he briefly worried he was heading toward Lesotho.

The experience required an overnight stay and assistance from local taxi rank operators to find his way.

Expanding Responsibilities and Innovation

Recognizing gaps in emergency healthcare services, Mr Mzimela advocated for and helped establish ambulance services in areas that previously lacked both vehicles and trained drivers. He personally operated ambulances, transporting critically ill patients to hospitals—an experience he found both challenging and rewarding. The ability to use emergency lights and respond rapidly to medical crises gave him deep satisfaction in directly serving community needs.

His role extended beyond healthcare logistics to include working with traditional healers, helping to formalize their education and certification processes. In the welfare division, he tackled the complex challenge of identity documentation. The absence of proper birth records meant many people had incorrect birth dates, creating complications for pension eligibility later in life. His team often had to make educated estimates of ages, highlighting the administrative challenges inherited from inadequate record-keeping systems.

Institutional Growth and Educational Leadership

In 1976, the office relocated to Ulundi, coinciding with the growth and restructuring of the Department of Community Affairs. The department eventually split into separate entities: the Department of Welfare and Pensions and the Department of Health, reflecting the expanding scope of government services.

Robert Mzimela

By 1977, Mr Mzimela identified a critical barrier to career advancement within the government: many assistant clerks possessed only Junior Certificate qualifications (equivalent to Grade 10), preventing their professional progression. He organized night classes to help these employees earn their matriculation certificates. Many of these individuals subsequently advanced to become full clerks and eventually Assistant Secretaries, including the late Rev. Khanyile of the Anglican Church in Ulundi.

Drawing on his educational background, Mr Mzimela volunteered to teach Zulu and Agricultural Science during lunch breaks and after work, demonstrating his commitment to both cultural preservation and practical education. His belief in the transformative power of education was evident in his observation that teachers and nurses were among the highest achievers in their communities.

Community Engagement and Educational Governance

Beyond his professional duties, Mr Mzimela actively participated in educational governance through school governing bodies. He served on the SGBs of Mahlabathini Primary and High School, and Masibumbane High School, institutions his own children attended. This involvement allowed him to influence educational policy at the grassroots level and ensure quality education for the next generation.

Even after retirement, his commitment to education continued through his participation in the SGB of Mehlathathani Primary School in Macekane, Empangeni—the same school where his aunt had taught, bringing his involvement full circle.

Appointment as Legislature Secretary

In March 1978, Mr Mzimela's career reached a significant milestone with his appointment as Secretary of the Legislative Assembly, a position that would define the remainder of his professional life and establish his legacy in South African governance. This role would encompass legislative functions, cultural preservation, and administrative leadership, shaping the development of KwaZulu and later KwaZulu-Natal.

As Secretary of the Legislative Assembly within the Chief Minister's Department, his role encompassed critical legislative functions, including the processing of laws and managing employee compensation systems.

Recognising the importance of legal expertise in his position, he pursued further education in 1985, completing a junior law degree (B.Juris) at the University of South Africa. This qualification proved invaluable as his responsibilities frequently required him to draft legislative proposals and provide guidance to legal counsel.

To enhance his administrative capabilities, Mr Mzimela undertook specialised training in 1988, completing a four-month public administration program at the prestigious Royal Institute of Public Administration in the United Kingdom. He supplemented this international experience with additional coursework at the University of Pretoria, where he focused on governmental systems through various administration courses, including an intensive six-week program in public management.

These educational pursuits reflected his commitment to professional development and equipped him with the theoretical foundations necessary to excel in his demanding role within the legislative framework. As Secretary of the Legislature, Mr Mzimela served as a key advisor to Prince Mangosuthu Buthelezi, proposing and drafting comprehensive plans for all legislative functions. His role extended far beyond administrative duties to encompass significant cultural and ceremonial responsibilities that honoured Zulu heritage and royal traditions.

Cultural and Royal Duties: He played a central role in preserving Zulu royal history, overseeing the unveiling of the tombs of revered monarchs, including King Mpande, King Cetshwayo, King Dinuzulu, and King Dingaan. His meticulous attention to detail was evident in his preparations for the KwaDlamahlahla grave unveiling and his procurement of suitable tombstones for senior princes and King Bhekuzulu. He also coordinated significant royal ceremonies, including arranging the marriages of uNdlunkulu uMaNdlovu and uNdlunkulu uMaMchiza.

Ceremonial and Public Functions: For many years, Mr. Mzimela supervised the prestigious uMkhosi Womhlanga (Reed Dance ceremony), demonstrating his deep understanding of Zulu cultural protocols. He orchestrated the grand opening of the Prince Mangosuthu Buthelezi Museum, creating a lasting tribute to the Chief Minister's legacy.

Administrative and Electoral Leadership: His organizational expertise extended to managing government Izimbizo (public meetings) in Durban and Johannesburg, including the complex logistics of renting buses and trains for public transport. He developed the foundational procedures for the Legislative Assembly opening - protocols that continue to be followed today. Additionally, he conducted elections for office holders and managed the distribution of results, working closely with the Chief Minister and the Speaker to ensure transparent electoral processes.

These diverse responsibilities reflected the unique nature of his position, where legislative expertise intersected with cultural stewardship and public administration.

Direct Accountability and Legislative Process: In his role overseeing legislative assembly operations and public functions, Mr Mzimela reported directly to Prince Mangosuthu Buthelezi, the Chief Minister—a position equivalent to today's Premier. A critical aspect of his responsibilities involved delivering enacted legislation to the national government in Pretoria, specifically to officials, including F.W. de Klerk and P.W. Botha. The process demanded excellence; any substandard work would result in unsigned documents being returned, requiring correction and resubmission. Air transport was utilized for these essential government communications between KwaZulu and Pretoria.

Administrative Structure and Staffing: Mr Mzimela managed a diverse team of support staff that included typists, drivers, interpreters, clerks, and messengers. This administrative infrastructure was essential for the smooth functioning of the legislative assembly. Among his notable appointments was Mr. Saunders, known as "Qili," the first white interpreter he hired who was fluent in Zulu. Mr. Saunders later advanced to serve as a magistrate in Durban, demonstrating the quality of personnel within the organization.

Urban Representation and Cultural Protection: The KwaZulu government maintained strategic offices in major urban centres, including Vereeniging, Welkom, Durban, Pietermaritzburg, Johannesburg, and Newcastle. These offices, overseen by elected urban representatives, served multiple functions: assisting hostel residents facing difficulties in white areas, particularly with employment issues, and representing Zulu interests across the province. This network represented a deliberate effort to protect and promote Zulu culture in urban environments where traditional support systems were often absent.

Community Service and Continued Development: Beyond his official duties, Mr Mzimela demonstrated commitment to community service through his founding membership in the Rotary Club, where he served until his retirement in 2004. The Rotary Club's initiatives included providing wheelchairs and essential equipment to communities in need, reflecting his dedication to social upliftment.

Following the 1994 democratic transition, Mr Mzimela continued his professional development by pursuing further studies at the University of the Witwatersrand under the new administration. He also contributed to educational advancement by participating in the planning process for the opening of Mangosuthu Technikon, demonstrating his ongoing commitment to institutional development even as the political landscape transformed.

Municipal Leadership in the 1980s

During the 1980s, Ulundi Municipality operated within strict budgetary constraints established by the Department of the Interior. The position of mayor was entirely voluntary, carrying significant responsibilities without financial compensation. The role encompassed comprehensive township management and the strategic allocation of funding to support various government activities.

In 1983, Mr Mzimela accepted the honour of becoming Ulundi's inaugural mayor during a period when the KwaZulu government-maintained oversight across all governance sectors. His appointment marked a pivotal moment in the township's development, as he assumed

responsibility for housing allocation and comprehensive urban planning.

Robert Mzimela

Urban Development and Infrastructure Planning

Mr Mzimela's primary mandate involved the systematic assignment of residential properties throughout Ulundi and the development of a coherent organizational framework for the growing township. His responsibilities extended to the practical task of naming streets and establishing essential commercial infrastructure. In consultation with Ithala Bank, he worked to identify the township's commercial needs.

When planning retail establishments, he advocated for OK stores over Spar, based on his assessment of community requirements and available resources.

Cultural and Community Events

Under his leadership, Ulundi became a vibrant centre for cultural activities. The township hosted significant events, including the Ingoma tournament, which drew participants from as far as Vryheid. September proved particularly meaningful, as the community gathered to commemorate King Shaka's Day, reinforcing the township's role as a cultural hub for the Zulu nation.

Residential Development Vision

The initial development phase focused on the A section houses, followed by the B-South residential areas. These properties were designed as four-bedroom family units, primarily intended to accommodate members of the Legislative Assembly and other government officials. Prince Mangosuthu Buthelezi championed an innovative architectural approach that deliberately diverged from the standardized, uniform appearance characteristic of most townships.

Prince Buthelezi's vision explicitly rejected the historical terminology of "locations," which carried negative connotations of labour compounds rather than dignified family neighbourhoods. Instead, he advocated for aesthetically distinctive homes that, while not necessarily luxurious, possessed unique design elements that reflected pride in community and cultural identity.

Community Living and Affordability

The township operated under a practical rent-paying system that made housing accessible to residents. Mr Mzimela himself embodied the community spirit of the era, sharing accommodations with three other individuals, with each contributor paying R3 toward the monthly rent. This arrangement reflected both the economic realities of the time and the collaborative approach that characterized early Ulundi's development.

Evolution of Ulundi's Residential Development

The housing development in Ulundi underwent a significant transformation from its original conception. What began as accommodation designed specifically for government personnel gradually evolved to serve a broader community as the township's population grew. This expansion reflected the

Robert Mzimela

organic development of Ulundi from a government administrative centre into a thriving residential community.

Property Ownership and Community-Centered Approach

The government adopted a progressive approach to property ownership that prioritized community welfare over profit maximization. While maintaining ownership of certain strategic properties, the administration made a deliberate decision to sell other residential units to community members at cost, based on the original construction expenses. This policy demonstrated a commitment to affordable homeownership and community empowerment rather than revenue generation.

Institutional Development and Adaptive Planning

The A section initially housed the first Ministerial residences, serving as the seat of government operations before the construction of the dedicated parliament building. The parliament complex was designed to accommodate both legislative functions and government offices under one roof, representing an efficient use of resources and space.

Educational Aspirations and Financial Realities

Following the completion of the parliament building, ambitious plans were developed to transform the former government offices in the A section into educational facilities. The vision encompassed a comprehensive college with designated areas for both hostels and classrooms, reflecting the government's commitment to expanding educational opportunities within the community.

However, these educational aspirations extended even further, with serious consideration given to establishing a full university within the existing infrastructure. These ambitious plans demonstrated the leadership's understanding of education as a cornerstone of community development and long-term prosperity.

Adaptation Despite Constraints

Unfortunately, financial limitations prevented the realization of both the college and university projects, highlighting the ongoing tension between visionary planning and fiscal realities. Despite these setbacks, the government offices in the A section continued to expand organically, adapting to meet the growing administrative needs of the various departments.

This pattern of growth and adaptation illustrated the dynamic nature of governance in Ulundi, where practical necessities often shaped development more than long-term strategic planning. The continued expansion, even amid funding challenges, demonstrated the resilience and adaptability that characterized the early years of Ulundi's development.

Conclusion: A Life of Service and Enduring Hope

In 2003, after nearly three decades of dedicated public service, Mr. M.R. Mzimela made the difficult decision to retire from government. The transition to the new democratic dispensation had brought with it challenges and philosophical differences that made it increasingly difficult for him to operate within the evolving governmental framework. Faced with these institutional changes, he chose to return to his agricultural roots, finding solace and purpose in farming—a pursuit that once again connected him to the land and the foundational values that had shaped his character.

From 1975 to 2003, Mr. Mzimela devoted the prime years of his professional life to a single, unwavering vision: the genuine improvement of the communities he served. Whether drafting legislation, organizing cultural ceremonies, developing Ulundi's infrastructure, or serving as the township's inaugural mayor, he approached each responsibility with wholehearted commitment and an authentic desire to uplift his people. His service transcended mere professional obligation; it represented a profound commitment to the ideals of progress, dignity, and community development.

Today, as he observes the current situation in South Africa, Mr Mzimela experiences the profound disappointment of a public servant who has witnessed the erosion of principles he spent decades trying to build. The energy, dedication, and institutional knowledge that he and his generation invested in creating functional, accountable governance appear to be dissipating before his eyes. The gap between the promises of liberation and the reality of contemporary South Africa weighs heavily on someone who sacrificed so much in the service of those very promises.

Yet despite no longer being active in public service, Mr. Mzimela has not abandoned hope for his country's future. He remains convinced that the vision of the Freedom Charter can still be realized, but only through fundamental changes in approach. He believes that the key lies in establishing the right education systems and ensuring that accurate, comprehensive information reaches all levels of society. With proper education and informed citizenry, he envisions a renewed collaboration between government and communities that could finally bridge the gap between the Charter's aspirations and South Africa's reality.

His life story serves as both a testament to the possibilities of dedicated public service and a reminder that achieving the Freedom Charter's vision requires more than good intentions—it demands sustained commitment, institutional integrity, and the active participation of educated, informed citizens working together toward common goals. In this respect, Mr Mzimela's legacy offers not just a historical account but a roadmap for those who still believe in the transformative potential of principled governance and community partnership.

Conclusion

Reflecting on the Journey: What Lies Ahead for South Africa?

The Zulu government, though short-lived, left a legacy of tangible development. In the early years, KwaZulu had fewer than ten high schools. Many learners could not even progress beyond Junior Certificate (Grade 10) because further education meant leaving home to attend expensive boarding schools. To address this, communities and the government worked together through a program known as "rand-for-rand": the community raised funds, and the government matched them to build new classrooms and schools. This enabled poor rural parents to send their children to school, while subsidized teachers' colleges allowed many to study teaching for as little as R1000 a year.

By the 1980s, initiatives under Prince Mangosuthu Buthelezi and traditional leaders had expanded access to education. TVET colleges built then are still in use today. Institutions like Comtech identified talented learners and prepared them to return and uplift their communities. Mangosuthu Technikon, established with the support of the Oppenheimer family, was created to expand access to higher education. Hospitals such as Prince Mshiyeni Memorial Hospital were also established under this government, alongside roads that were regularly maintained — even gravel roads in rural areas.

Unlike other homelands such as Transkei and Ciskei, KwaZulu initially resisted accepting "homeland" status but eventually used it strategically to drive development. By 1994, KwaZulu had saved enough money to sustain governance for five years, a remarkable achievement compared to the financial struggles of other territories. The administration actively promoted education: workers were supported to attend universities, many became magistrates and judges, and students were even refunded for passing their exams. Promotion in the workplace was tied to academic achievement, creating a culture of advancement and accountability.

Today, by contrast, such structures of encouragement have disappeared. Opportunities that once uplifted communities have been replaced by stagnation.

South African politics has since become the low-hanging fruit for personal enrichment. Parliament, once envisioned as a space for public service, has become a costly drain on the nation. Members of Parliament travel in blue-light convoys, claim travel and daily allowances on top of their salaries, and spend countless hours in sessions that too often end in political bickering rather than solutions.

Even the very design of Parliament reveals waste. Under the old system, Parliament sat six months in Cape Town and six months in Pretoria. Today, it remains year-round in Cape Town, necessitating the state to fund ongoing travel, accommodation, and allowances. This is money that could be redirected to development. A practical solution would be to confine Parliament's sittings to a set period, after which MPs should return to their constituencies to work directly with communities and understand their struggles.

If South Africa is serious about building a future aligned with the Freedom Charter, it must cut unnecessary expenditure, re-establish accountability, and place the needs of ordinary citizens above political privilege.

1. Why Parliament Sittings Cost Money

Every sitting of Parliament in South Africa carries costs:

- Salaries and allowances: Members of Parliament (MPs) earn high salaries, sitting allowances, travel and accommodation reimbursements.

- Operational costs: Running the chambers (security, staff, utilities, translation services, printing of documents, catering).

- Travel and logistics: Many MPs travel from other provinces to Cape Town at great expense, while most government offices remain in Pretoria.

- Special sittings: Extra sessions or late sittings mean overtime payments for staff.

So, the idea of restricting sittings is really about whether fewer sittings = less expenditure.

2. Potential Ways to Reduce Spending

a) Reduce Sitting Schedules

- Consolidate debates and votes into fewer sessions.

- Reduce ceremonial sittings.

- Utilize technology (video conferencing, hybrid meetings) instead of flying everyone to Cape Town frequently.

b) Reduce Operational Costs

- Limit the budget for luxury perks such as business-class flights, hotel stays, and car allowances.

- Restrict the use of public money for non-essential catering, events, and international parliamentary trips.

c) Reconsider the Location of Parliament

- Instead of building from scratch, South Africa could utilise existing infrastructure from the old KwaZulu Legislative Assembly in Ulundi, which was previously home to parliamentary activity. This would reduce the need for expensive construction and redirect funds toward development.

- Beyond location, Parliament should also adjust its working hours: starting earlier in the day and extending sittings into the evening where necessary. This would shorten the overall parliamentary calendar, minimising unnecessary days in session and lowering cumulative costs.

d) Reduce the Size of Parliament

- South Africa has 400 MPs in the National Assembly and 90 in the National Council of Provinces (NCOP). This is quite large relative to the population size. Reducing the number of MPs could lower long-term salary and operational expenses.

e) Digitization and Efficiency

- Move toward a more digitized operation to reduce travel and printing costs.

- Cap perks and allowances.

- Combine structural reforms (a smaller Parliament, relocation, and hybrid sittings) with efficiency improvements in scheduling.

Why Do We Kill Our Councillors?

Inflation of salaries

When the ANC took over in 1994, one of the first major changes was the increase in salaries compared to those of the old legislative assemblies. Members of the KwaZulu Legislative Assembly, for example, earned around R2,000 a month in the early 1990s. By 1994, this was raised to R15,000 a month—a jump that, in today's value, is equivalent to moving from about R15,000 to over R114,000. This widening gap created the impression that Parliament was no longer about service, but about employment and enrichment. Suddenly, politics became a career path: everyone wanted to sit in Parliament, everyone wanted to be a councillor.

But it was not always this way. In the earlier years, councillors were not salaried career politicians but community servants. They worked for the development of the people, not for financial gain. Councillors acted as liaisons between the government and the community, convening meetings, listening to grievances, and carrying those concerns to the authorities. Their value lay in service, not status.

As a councillor of Ulundi from 1983 to 1989, I was not paid a salary. Only later was I given a token stipend of R12 per month—an amount so small that it could hardly cover anything, and in today's value amounts to almost nothing. All travel costs and duties were carried from my own pocket, without compensation. Yet the work was done, driven by the love of my country and a desire for community development, not by the promise of financial reward.

During apartheid, of course, white South Africans elected their councillors and municipal officials under a segregated system. These councils controlled well-funded municipalities with access to modern infrastructure, housing, and services— privileges denied to Black communities. Representation and voting rights were reserved for whites, giving them full control over local government in "white areas." However, even under these conditions, Black councillors worked with very little, motivated by a desire to serve rather than wealth.

Escalating crime is another proof of failure in our government

South Africa's organized crime is shocking—and what's even more shocking is the alleged involvement of some of our political leaders in drug cartel networks. They act as conduits, ensuring the smooth operation of these syndicates, hiding in plain sight as people we are supposed to trust. Our country seems to be taking a dangerous turn, with politicians repeatedly mentioned in the drug trade. This might explain the deafening silence around illegal immigrants and notorious drug dealers getting away with murder. How can we hope to eradicate crime if the very people tasked with protecting us are also benefiting from these heinous acts?

The freedom charter clearly states: "All Shall Be Equal Before the Law!" Yet that principle seems distant, as so many criminals evade justice. Inanda is notorious as one of the country's most dangerous areas, and we saw Lieutenant-General Nhlanhla Mkhwanazi trying to confront crime there. But those who speak out are often forced out of their positions, with dirt dug up to tarnish their reputation and discourage them.

Comments and Conclusions

1. Promoting Empowerment through Cooperative Training and Personal Development

Integrate continuous cooperative training sessions into the primary and secondary school curricula to equip youth with entrepreneurial skills and continually update the curriculum to meet the community's evolving needs effectively.

Additionally, educate students about their personal character traits, strengths, and weaknesses to foster their personal growth and development. This aspect is crucial for entrepreneurs to carve out a niche and foster innovation.

Partner with non-profit organizations to empower individuals to achieve their full potential. Our society is facing a crisis of self-identity, as shown by the rising rates of youth suicide stemming from the competitiveness propagated by social media.

Offer ongoing training to stokvel groups to motivate them to establish businesses that can generate employment opportunities, rather than solely buying food.

2. Instilling the Spirit of "Ubuntu "and Strong Work Ethics for Youth Success:

Advocate for values of cooperation, inclusivity, and self-improvement to foster a culture of mutual respect within our communities.

Encourage a shift in mindset away from seeking instant gratification and quick wealth towards a mentality of working hard rather than just working smart. Emphasize the importance of discipline, hard work, and perseverance for sustainable personal and economic growth. By instilling a culture of hard work, we can also contribute to reducing crime in our communities. As the first generation of freedom, we must exert extra effort to establish a lasting legacy and pave the way for future generations.

Furthermore, let's draw inspiration from Kenya and other successful cooperative models by sending youth to learn and adopt effective work ethics and practices.

3. Addressing the shortage of water in South Africa:

Given the scarcity of water, particularly in rural areas, pit toilets are unavoidable. Embracing this fact, we must now focus on how to effectively reduce the risks associated with the use of pit toilets.

To mitigate the risk of accidents, we propose equipping toilet seats with additional support or safety measures, such as supporting handles to prevent children from falling into the toilets, ensuring their safety while using the facilities.

Recognizing the challenge of water scarcity for flushing toilets, it is important to explore innovative solutions to maintain hygiene and prevent the spread of infectious diseases

One practical approach could involve the development of affordable chemical solutions that can be added to toilets after use to dissolve waste and eliminate harmful bacteria, such as *E. coli.* -This method could help conserve water resources while ensuring proper sanitation standards in pit toilets.

Installing ground reservoirs to collect rainwater in public spaces can enhance water access for local communities and promote sustainable water management practices.

4. Addressing Water Scarcity in Schools in Rural Areas:

Providing self-sustaining water sources for schools by installing ground reservoirs that collect rainwater from the building.

Supporting schools in establishing their water sources can enhance water security and reliability for educational institutions.

Subsidizing Jojo tanks for rural households -Offering subsidies for water storage solutions can help disadvantaged households secure access to clean water and build resilience against water system failures

5. Employing an infection control person for school hygiene:

To promote a clean and healthy environment in schools, we recommend hiring an infection control specialist who can oversee sanitation practices and ensure adherence to hygiene standards.

Training an assistant nurse for this role, who can be compensated at a lower rate, would be cost-effective while ensuring that the cleaner at the school adheres to proper cleaning routines and educates students on hand hygiene practices and the prevention of waterborne diseases.

The infection control person can play a crucial role in preventing outbreaks of infectious diseases by monitoring school conditions, identifying potential risks early, coordinating with health district teams for timely interventions, and reporting notifiable medical conditions directly to NICD.

By proactively managing hygiene and sanitation practices in schools, we can safeguard the health of students and create a safer learning environment for everyone.

6. Enhancing Government Communication with Communities

South African media and politicians have a responsibility to ensure that news, manifestos, and important information are inclusive and accessible to all citizens. Currently, much of the content disseminated through platforms such as social media, television, radio, and newspapers does not cater to the country's diverse population. Messaging is often delivered in only a few languages, leaving large portions of the public without access to critical updates. To address this, all governmental announcements, policy updates, and media coverage should be made available in South Africa's 11 official languages. This approach would ensure that people from all backgrounds, regardless of education level or linguistic ability, can understand and engage with important information.

Clear, concise, and simple communication is essential. Messages should be presented in a way that is easy to comprehend for individuals of all ages, including children, and public speakers should convey information with clarity, pace, and eloquence. During events such as the COVID-19 pandemic, communities often turned to influential figures for guidance when official communication was unclear or inaccessible. By making media and political communication inclusive, South Africa can promote understanding, participation, and trust across all communities.

7. Subsidizing Electricity for Farmers

Drawing from personal experience, I understand the impact of high electricity costs on farming businesses. Due to the exorbitant expenses, I was unable to sustain my farming operation, leading to the unfortunate retrenchment of 20 employees. The soaring electricity prices not only affected my livelihood but also had ripple effects, causing losses for vendors and even prompting schools to seek produce from external sources. This setback had grave consequences for the community of eMtunzini, resulting in significant job losses.

Reflecting on the period before 2010, when electricity rates were more conducive for irrigation purposes, it was notably easier for farmers to utilize electricity efficiently. However, during President Zuma's tenure, additional daily rates were introduced, significantly impacting agricultural operations. This change led to increased financial burdens on farmers, making it challenging to sustain their businesses and resulting in repercussions such as the retrenchment of employees.

By implementing subsidies on electricity for farmers, not only can the financial strain on agricultural enterprises be alleviated, but it can also bolster food security and contribute to making produce more affordable for consumers. This measure would not only support farmers in sustaining their operations but also benefit consumers by ensuring a stable and affordable food supply.

8. Fire Mitigation Strategies for Informal Settlements

To prevent devastating fires that inflict heavy losses on informal settlements, such as the recent incident in Cape Town, where over 700 families were left homeless, a proactive plan must be established. One effective approach is for the government to supply automatic fire-fighting balls to these settlements. These innovative devices can swiftly suppress fires, reducing the need for extensive rebuilding and minimizing the number of affected homes. They are especially beneficial for individuals who may struggle to operate traditional fire extinguishers.

Additionally, it is essential to educate communities on fire safety and firefighting techniques. For instance, in combating fires in sugar cane farming, the use of pump bottles containing a mixture of washing powder and water has been effective. Providing training on the proper utilization of these tools can empower residents to promptly respond to fires and protect their homes and families from the devastating impact of such disasters.

9. Cultivating Future Farmers through Practical Agricultural Education

Nurturing agricultural sustainability from the ground up, the decline in agriculture and the lack of farmers owning farms in KwaZulu-Natal present a significant challenge. To revitalize the agricultural sector, it is crucial to introduce practical agriculture education at a young age, starting from primary school. By engaging youth in hands-on agricultural activities such as growing crops and raising livestock, we can instil a sense of passion and practical skills in farming. This approach can be particularly impactful in rural settings, where many people rely on social grants for their livelihood. Empowering youth to farm can not only provide them with a means of self-sufficiency but also contribute to reducing food costs by producing their own food and vegetables.

South Africa's journey since 1994 has been marked by both progress and painful regression. The Freedom Charter promised dignity, equality, and justice, yet decades later, inequality, corruption, and weak institutions continue to frustrate those aspirations. The examples drawn from history—whether the failures of land reform, the lessons of the KwaZulu government, or the struggles of grassroots activism—show that leadership without integrity always ends in betrayal.

But this story is not only one of failure; it is also one of possibility. Civil society movements, ordinary citizens, and committed leaders have shown that change is possible when accountability, community partnership, and service to the people take precedence over personal gain. As the Freedom Charter proclaimed, **"The People Shall Govern!"**—a vision that remains as urgent today as it was in 1955, reminding us that true progress comes when those who serve remember whom they serve.

The road ahead will not be easy. It requires cutting wasteful governance, rebuilding institutions, empowering youth, and restoring trust between citizens and the state. It demands a new culture of responsibility—one where the promises of democracy are no longer hollow, but lived realities for all.

The task belongs not only to the government but to every citizen who still believes in the vision of the Freedom Charter. If we can rekindle the spirit of collective struggle, prioritize education, and insist on accountability, South Africa can yet become the nation its founders dreamed of—a country where freedom, dignity, and equality are not just constitutional rights, but everyday truths.

Aluta continua—the struggle continues, but so does the hope

References

Luescher, T.M., Loader, L. & Mugume, T. (2017). #FeesMustFall: An Internet-age student movement in South Africa and the case of the University of the Free State. Politikon, 44(2), pp.231–245.

Pithouse, R. (2013). Abahlali baseMjondolo and the struggle for the city in South Africa. International Journal of Urban and Regional Research, 37(3), pp.1020–1036.

Langa, M. (2017). #Hashtag: An analysis of the #FeesMustFall Movement at South African universities. Johannesburg: Centre for the Study of Violence and Reconciliation.

Moyo, S. (2011). Three decades of agrarian reform in Zimbabwe. Journal of Peasant Studies, 38(3), pp.493–531

Fraser, A. & Lungu, J. (2007). For Whom the Windfalls? Winners and Losers in the Privatisation of Zambia's Copper Mines. Lusaka: Civil Society Trade Network of Zambia.

The Ongoing Struggle for the Vision of the Freedom Charter

Lessons from the KwaZulu Government Legacy

The brief but impactful existence of the KwaZulu Government offers instructive lessons about what effective governance can achieve when properly focused and resourced. Despite its short lifespan, this administration accomplished remarkable transformations in education and infrastructure that continue to benefit communities today.

When the KwaZulu Government began its work, KwaZulu-Natal had fewer than ten high schools. Most students could not progress beyond Junior Certificate (Grade 10) due to financial constraints and the requirement to leave home for boarding school education. The government's innovative "rand-for-rand" program, where government and community contributions matched each other, enabled the construction of numerous schools that brought quality education to rural areas previously underserved.

Teacher training colleges were heavily subsidized, with annual fees of approximately R1,000, making education accessible to aspiring educators. The establishment of the University of Zululand stands as a testament to community collaboration—traditional leaders donated cattle, the Mzimela family contributed land, and various community members pooled resources to create this institution of higher learning.

Infrastructure development under the KwaZulu Government included well-maintained roads, both provincial routes like the R102 and smaller roads serviced by graders. Technical and Vocational Education and Training (TVET) colleges that continue to operate today were established during this period. Institutions like Comtech specifically recruited talented students with the expectation that they would return to serve their communities after graduation.

The government's foresight extended to healthcare, with the construction of facilities like Prince Mshiyeni Memorial Hospital, while working alongside missionary-established healthcare centers. The collaboration with private sector leaders like Oppenheimer to establish Mangosuthu Technikon demonstrated effective public-private partnerships.

Perhaps most significantly, the KwaZulu Government's approach to education created lasting change. Workers were encouraged to pursue university education, with government reimbursement for successful completion of studies. Many individuals from this era went on to become magistrates, judges, and other professionals. The B.Juris degree program provided accessible legal education, with successful students receiving financial support that incentivized academic achievement.

The Cost of Contemporary Governance

The contrast between past achievements and current expenditure patterns reveals concerning priorities in democratic South Africa. Parliamentary operations have become increasingly expensive, with Members of Parliament receiving substantial salaries, sitting allowances, travel reimbursements, and accommodation costs. The decision to maintain year-round Parliamentary sessions in Cape Town, rather than the original six-month rotation between Cape Town and Pretoria, has significantly increased operational costs.

The financial burden includes security, staff, utilities, translation services, document printing, and catering for Parliamentary chambers. The geographic separation between Parliament in Cape Town and most government departments in Pretoria creates additional travel and accommodation expenses. Special sessions and extended sittings generate overtime payments for support staff, further inflating costs.

Several practical reforms could reduce these expenditures: consolidating debates and votes into fewer sessions, utilizing technology for hybrid meetings rather than requiring physical presence, limiting luxury perks such as business-class travel, and reconsidering the location of Parliament to reduce duplication of services. The current structure, with 400 MPs in the National Assembly and 90 in the National Council of Provinces, is disproportionately large relative to South Africa's population and could benefit from reduction.

The Crisis of Local Government

The transformation of local government from community service to lucrative employment has contributed to the crisis facing municipal councillors. Under the previous system, legislative assembly members earned R2,000 monthly, but post-1994 salaries jumped to R15,000, creating the perception that government service is primarily about personal enrichment rather than public service.

Historical context reveals that councillors once served as unpaid liaisons between communities and government, holding meetings to address residents' concerns and advocate for their needs. During Mr. Mzimela's tenure as mayor from 1983-1988, he received R12 monthly, yet the work was accomplished through dedication to community development rather than financial motivation.

The current crisis, where councillors face intimidation and violence, stems partly from the high stakes associated with positions that now provide substantial financial benefits and access to resources.

This has transformed local politics into highly contested terrain where positions become worth fighting—and sometimes killing—for.

Crime, Corruption, and the Rule of Law

The Freedom Charter's promise that "**All Shall be Equal Before the Law**" remains unfulfilled as South Africa grapples with organized crime networks allegedly involving political leaders. The integration of politicians into drug cartels and criminal syndicates represents a fundamental betrayal of public trust and explains the seeming inability to address certain criminal activities effectively.

The establishment of commissions of inquiry to address these issues has proven ineffective, consuming state resources without producing meaningful accountability or arrests. The pattern of investigating wrongdoing through lengthy processes that rarely result in consequences has eroded public confidence in democratic institutions.

Areas like Inanda, recognized among the world's most dangerous, illustrate the failure of the state to provide basic security for its citizens. When law enforcement officials like General Mkhwanazi attempt to address these challenges directly, they face institutional resistance and personal attacks designed to discredit their efforts.

Cultural Identity and Institutional Capacity

The erosion of cultural confidence manifests in subtle but significant ways throughout South African society. The automatic switch to English in any gathering that includes non-African participants reflects a deep-seated belief that African languages and cultural practices are insufficient for serious discourse. This linguistic deference suggests an incomplete decolonization of the mind that undermines authentic self-determination.

The abandonment of agricultural practices and communal support systems in favor of total dependence on government services has weakened community resilience. Traditional skills in farming, construction, and local economic development have atrophied as communities wait for external intervention rather than mobilizing internal resources.

The Challenge of Leadership and Vision

Post-apartheid leadership has often prioritized short-term personal gain over long-term national development. The mindset of "getting while the getting is good" reflects insecurity about the permanence of political power and a failure to appreciate the responsibilities that come with democratic authority.

The result has been economic stagnation, rising unemployment, and increasing dependence on foreign assistance. Recent developments, such as the reduction of USAID funding due to shifting American priorities, highlight South Africa's vulnerability to external policy changes and the urgent need for sustainable, self-reliant development strategies.

A Path Forward: Education, Accountability, and Renewal

Despite these challenges, the vision of the Freedom Charter remains achievable through committed leadership and institutional reform. The foundation for progress lies in education systems that prepare citizens for both economic participation and civic engagement. Information must flow freely to all levels of society, enabling informed decision-making and democratic accountability.

The collaboration between government and communities that characterized the KwaZulu period demonstrates that effective governance is possible when leaders prioritize service over self-enrichment. Technical solutions exist for most of South Africa's challenges; what remains elusive is the political will to implement them consistently and transparently.

Faith and Determination

The biblical reminder from Deuteronomy 28:43-44 serves as both warning and motivation: "The foreigner who lives among you will rise higher and higher, but you will sink lower and lower. He will lend to you, but you will not lend to him. He will be the head, and you will be the tail." This scripture calls for national self-examination and renewed commitment to the principles that should govern a sovereign people.

South Africa's future depends not on external validation or assistance, but on the willingness of its citizens to reclaim the ideals that motivated the liberation struggle. The Freedom Charter's vision of a non-racial democracy where all people share in the country's wealth remains a worthy goal, but achieving it requires moving beyond the rhetoric of transformation to the hard work of building accountable institutions and fostering civic responsibility.

The Continuing Struggle

As the liberation slogan reminds us: Aluta continua—the struggle continues. The struggle today is not against apartheid but against the corruption, inefficiency, and lack of vision that prevent South Africa from realizing its potential. Success requires citizens who are willing to demand excellence from their leaders and leaders who are willing to serve with integrity and competence.

The choice facing South Africa is clear: continue on the current trajectory toward further decline, or recommit to the principles of the Freedom Charter with the dedication, planning, and sacrifice that meaningful transformation requires. The future of the country—and the hope of fulfilling the promises made to previous generations—depends on the decisions made today.

With faith in the resilience of the South African people and confidence in the enduring relevance of the Freedom Charter's vision, there remains reason for hope. But hope must be accompanied by action, and action must be guided by the recognition that the responsibility for South Africa's future lies not with external forces, but with South Africans themselves.

The journey toward the Freedom Charter's realization continues. The question is whether current and future generations will prove worthy of the sacrifices made by those who came before, and whether they will leave a legacy that honors both the struggles of the past and the possibilities of the future.

A Message to Future Generations

From Mr. Muntuwekosi Robert Mzimela

My dear children of South Africa, you must forgive this old man for taking up your time with another lengthy speech. But when you have lived nearly eight decades and spent twenty-eight of those years trying to serve your people, you accumulate a few thoughts that refuse to stay quiet—like an old rooster that still thinks it must crow at dawn.

I have witnessed South Africa in more forms than a chameleon changes colours—from the structured but unjust apartheid system, through the promising years of the KwaZulu Government (when even a grey old man like me could become a mayor!), to the euphoria of 1994's democratic transition, and now the troubling realities of our current state. From this vantage point of having lived through these transformations—and survived to tell the tale—I offer you these reflections.

The Power of Education and Self-Reliance

I was the first in my family to earn a university degree—quite an achievement for a country boy who once got lost trying to deliver medicine to Ezakheni Clinic and nearly ended up in Lesotho! That education opened doors not just for me, but for

171

countless others who followed. Education remains your most powerful weapon against poverty, ignorance, and manipulation. But let it be education that teaches you to think critically, not just to memorize and repeat like a well-trained parrot.

Learn your history, understand your Constitution, and never allow anyone to convince you that you are not capable of excellence. We once built schools with our own hands, contributed our cattle to establish universities, and created institutions that served our communities effectively. If this grey old man and his generation could do that with limited resources, imagine what you can accomplish with all the tools at your disposal!

The Responsibility of Leadership

I have seen leadership that served and leadership that merely enriched itself. I have watched how the promise of public service can either transform communities or become a pathway to personal wealth. When your time comes to lead— and it will come in various forms,remember that true leadership is sacrifice, not privilege.

The leaders of my generation in the KwaZulu period understood that our role was to serve our people, not to be served by them. We earned modest salaries—I received R12 per month as mayor, barely enough to buy a decent pair of shoes! But we built lasting institutions. We invested in future generations rather than in our own immediate comfort. This grey old man never owned a blue light vehicle or travelled in luxury, yet I can point to schools and roads that still serve our people today. This is the standard by which you must measure those who seek to lead you, and the standard you must uphold when you lead others.

Cultural Pride and Practical Progress

Never be ashamed of who you are or where you come from. I have watched our people struggle with an inferiority complex that makes us switch to English the moment we want to be taken seriously. Your mother tongue is not inferior to any language on earth. Your cultural practices are not primitive customs to be discarded in pursuit of modernity.

Yet, do not let cultural pride become an excuse for rejecting beneficial knowledge or useful innovations from other cultures. The goal is not to return to the past unchanged, but to build a future that honours your heritage while embracing the tools and knowledge needed for progress.

Demanding Accountability

You have inherited a democracy that previous generations died to secure. Do not treat it carelessly. Your vote is not a favour you do for politicians—it is a responsibility you owe to your children and to those who sacrificed for your freedom.

When you see corruption, expose it. When you witness incompetence, challenge it. When you encounter injustice, resist it. But do so with facts, with courage, and with the understanding that change requires sustained effort, not just momentary outrage.

The Vision Remains Valid

The Freedom Charter that inspired our struggle for liberation was not naive idealism—it was a practical blueprint for a just society. When it declared that "The People Shall Govern" and "All Shall Share in the Country's Wealth," it was describing achievable goals, not impossible dreams.

The failure to realize these ideals fully does not invalidate them. It simply means that each generation must take up the work anew, applying the lessons of previous failures and building on the foundations laid by those who came before.

Economic Self-Determination

Learn to build wealth, not just to spend it. Understand how businesses work, how money flows, and how economic systems function. The prosperity you seek will not come from government grants or foreign charity—it will come from your own knowledge, skills, and determination to create value for others.

Support each other's enterprises, invest in your communities, and never accept that poverty is your permanent condition. You have the same intellectual capacity as any people on earth. Use it.

The Long View

I am now in my twilight years, but you are in your dawn. The problems that seem overwhelming today are not permanent features of South African life—they are challenges that can be overcome by people with the will and wisdom to address them systematically.

Do not expect change to happen quickly or easily. The institutions we built during the KwaZulu period took years to establish and required the cooperation of many people with different skills and resources. Similarly, the South Africa you want to see will require patience, planning, and persistence.

A Personal Challenge

I challenge you to be better than my generation in the choices you make and the standards you set. Learn from our successes and our failures, but do not be limited by them. You have access to knowledge, technology, and opportunities that we could only dream of when I was starting my career—when this grey old man thought a telephone was advanced technology!

Use these advantages not just to improve your own lives, but to lift up your communities and your country. Make the sacrifices necessary to build something lasting, something that your own children will thank you for creating. And hopefully, when you reach my age, you'll have fewer grey hairs from worrying about the state of the country!

Faith and Determination

Finally, maintain your faith—whether in God, in your ancestors, in your community, or in the fundamental goodness of human nature. Cynicism is easy, but it is also barren. Hope combined with action is what transforms societies.

The struggle for justice, dignity, and prosperity did not end in 1994—it simply entered a new phase. Your generation must take up that struggle with the same courage and determination that your predecessors showed, but with the wisdom that comes from understanding both the possibilities and the pitfalls of power.

South Africa's greatest days can still lie ahead, but only if you have the courage to demand them and the wisdom to build them. The Freedom Charter's promise remains: this country belongs to all who live in it. Make sure that promise becomes reality for your children and their children.

The future is in your hands. Use it wisely.

Muntuwenkosi Robert Mzimela

Former Secretary of the KwaZulu Legislature

First Mayor of Ulundi

Son of the Soil, Servant of the People

Witness To Leadership

I will forever be indebted to Mr M. R. Mzimela, the author of this book, for his immense contribution to my highly successful employment life. I started working for the erstwhile KwaZulu Government in 1973. From then until 1981, I worked for the Department of Community Affairs, which later morphed into the Department of Interior.

In 1981, Mr Robert Mzimela, then Secretary for the KwaZulu Legislative Assembly, created a new post for a Public Relations Officer. The purpose of the role was to inform visitors about Zulu history, the inner workings of the KwaZulu Government, and to educate them on local tourist attractions such as the partly reconstructed King Cetshwayo's Royal Palace. I passed the interview and was appointed to the post.

I would host tourists, mainly from overseas countries such as Australia, the United States, Britain, and New Zealand. Local school children and their teachers would also visit the sites, and I would explain the significance of these historic locations to them in detail.

I soon felt that I could do more in the field of public relations rather than spending long periods waiting for visitors. I consulted with Mr Robert Mzimela and expressed my interest in gaining more knowledge in the field. Although he had not been comprehensively exposed to public relations and did not have the information I required, he encouraged me to pursue further learning and gather as much knowledge as possible for the potential expansion of the Public Relations Division I oversaw.

At this stage, it is important to mention that, apart from hosting delegations of visitors, I also officiated in the proceedings of the Legislative Assembly. I then approached Mr Jordan, who was Mr Mzimela's supervisor, and enquired about public relations in its entirety and how we could establish a more comprehensive model that would strengthen the relationship between the KwaZulu Government, overseas countries, and the news media. He informed me that he was unsure about public relations.

I later learnt about a Public Relations course offered at Damelin in Durban and wished to enrol. I visited Mr Mzimela to enquire about furthering my education. Not only did he give me permission, but he also encouraged me to continue. It was a six-month post-matric Public Relations course held on weekends.

I completed the course and received my certificate. The course gave me exposure to public relations activities within and outside the Government framework. Although the theory was useful, I still felt the need to understand the practical aspects of the field. I learnt of a company in Durban, The Durban Publicity Association, which promoted the image of Durban to tourists.

With Mr Mzimela's approval, I visited the Director, who welcomed me warmly and explained how his department was run. He suggested that I also visit the Public Relations Officer at the Durban Municipality. I did so, and once again I was received warmly and given a detailed explanation of their operations.

I then visited the Natal Technikon (now known as DUT – Durban University of Technology) and sought the attention of the Head of Public Relations. He did not hesitate to provide a thorough explanation of what he taught his students. When I returned to Ulundi, I had a full understanding of Public Relations. I must emphasise that I would not have gained any of this knowledge without the permission and support of my supervisor, Mr Robert Mzimela.

With the information I had gathered, I drafted a memorandum to Cabinet, endorsed by Mr Mzimela, proposing the establishment of a comprehensive Public Relations Branch known as the "KwaZulu Bureau of Communication." The Cabinet approved the submission, and I was appointed Acting Director of the new division.

I want to state clearly that all that I achieved—some of which even received praise from politicians—is a product of Mr Mzimela's character. I attribute the creation and existence of the KwaZulu, and later the KwaZulu-Natal, Bureau of Communication to Mr M. R. Mzimela. He will remain my perpetual mentor, leader, and influencer. Had he not recruited me and supported my ideas, the Bureau of Communication would never have existed. I owe my entire career—from the time I became a Public Relations Officer to my roles as Chief

Robert Mzimela

Public Relations Officer, Public Relations Officer for two Premiers, and Director in His Majesty the King's Department, to Mr M. R. Mzimela.

TC Memela

Gallery

M.R. Mzimela, LLB—a moment of achievement and hope for what the law could deliver for South Africa.

With wife and four grandchildren. The legacy continues through the next generation.

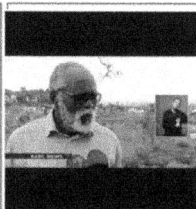

Speaking to SABC News as family spokesperson after the passing of iNkosi Mpiyezintombi Mzimela. Honoring a leader and relative.

Celebrating Dr. Ntokozo Mzimela's graduation as a medical specialist, 2019. The dreams we fought for, achieved by the next generation.

M.R. Mzimela on his LLB graduation with his wife, four children and secretary Zakhona- a family of achievement built on sacrifice and hope.

My father, Phambumbayo Mzimela. A man whose strength and values shaped everything I became.

Thanksgiving dinner upon retirement with his wife. A moment of reflection after decades of service.

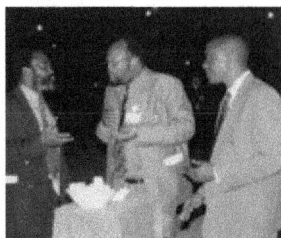

With colleagues at a gathering in the UK, late 1980s.

A Daughter's Reflection

Dr. Ntokozo Mzimela: Pathologist, Global Health Icon & Ambassador President (Africa Health Excellence Organization)

Baba, being your daughter has been the greatest blessing I could ever ask for. I thank God every day for the gift of you. From your character, I have drawn strength and inspiration—your unconditional love, sharp wit, humility, tireless work ethic, and generous spirit have shaped who I am.

Receiving an award in London in 2023—the very city where you once had the opportunity to study—felt like a full circle moment. That achievement was dedicated to you, a testament to your unwavering support and guidance. You have been our steadfast pillar, a true gentleman in every sense.

I pray that South Africa embraces you warmly and that many will draw from your deep well of wisdom. I am because you are.

Mnguni, Donda, Lwandle kaluwelwa liwelwa yizinkonjane zona ezindizela phezulu (clan names)

A Genealogical List of the

Mzimela Chieftainship

Sihubele (±1820–1840)

↓

Sigodo (±1840–1870)

↓

Zimema (±1885–1920)

appointed by King Cetshwayo

↓

Ntshidi (±1920–1944)

↓

Mpindelwa Dindi (±1944–1946)

regent

↓

Lindelihle (1946–±1992)

↓

Mpiyezintombi (±1992–2014)

↓

Thanduyise (2015–present)

Leadership Heritage

of the Mzimela Chieftainship

Three Generations of Excellence that Shaped Robert's Statesmanship

1. Zimema (±1885-1920): Nation-Building & Strategic Vision

Zimema was *"a conspicuous star in the clan"* who rebuilt the AbakwaMzimela to prominence after absorption into Shaka's army, incorporating displaced groups to transform a fragmented clan into a unified force. Appointed senior chief overseeing seven tribes, officials called him *"one of our best chiefs"*—demonstrating the strategic nation-building essential for statesmanship.

2. Ntshidi (±1920-1944): Progressive Vision & Education Advocacy

Despite colonial restrictions, Ntshidi applied in 1939 to establish the Zimema Memorial School. When rejected, he reapplied in 1940, promising to accommodate *"both heathens and christians."* His persistence revealed understanding that education was key to advancement—the same value driving Robert's ability to analyze complex governance in *Broken Promises*.

3. Lindelihle (1946-±1980s): Diplomatic Skill & Collaborative Governance

Lindelihle and Chief Muntukanakudla settled the longstanding Mzimela-Mkhwanazi boundary dispute *"quickly and easier"* than predecessors. His governance earned increasing trust—his annual bonus grew from R6 to R54 for *"helpful contribution."* This demonstrated ability to work within existing systems while maintaining his people's interests—a hallmark of effective statesmanship.

Conclusion: These leadership qualities—strategic nation-building, commitment to education, and diplomatic collaboration—flow through the Mzimela chieftainship. Robert's ability to write *Broken Promises* with penetrating insight reflects this inherited wisdom of rebuilding after crisis, recognizing education's transformative power, and navigating complex political systems with integrity.

www.ingramcontent.com/pod-product-compliance
Lightning Source LLC
Chambersburg PA
CBHW052112030426
42335CB00025B/2951